G000037774

'People who get "l[...]
relate to the mes[...]
reserved for sunse[...]
otherwise. In this h[...]
our eyes to wonder in the most unlikely people and
places. And a good job too, or what's the incarnation
all about?'

Ian Stackhouse, pastor and writer

'A truly magical book that invites us to recapture the
wide-eyed wonder of childhood, to reconnect with
the power of wonder, and to rediscover the mystery
of God incarnate. Morris's poetic reflections lift us
above the mundane while opening up the possibility
of everyday miracles – and finding God in ordinary
and unexpected places. This beautiful book speaks
poignantly to the heart and leaves you with the
sense of having found something precious that you
had lost along the way.'

Kate Nicholas, author, broadcaster and preacher

'Steve Morris's enthralling book begins where the
frontiers of most human imaginations end.

'He has the spiritual and literary originality to take his
readers on journeys of theophany – encounters with
God – which travel from a lecture theatre at Charing
Cross Hospital to outer space with an astronaut, to

grieving donkeys and to experiences with every day saints.

'Marinated in prayer and Scripture, Steve's writings are to the divine experience what David Attenborough's programmes are to the natural world. Both offer revelations to which expressions of wonder are the inevitable reaction, reminiscent of St Francis of Assisi falling to his knees crying "My God and my all!"

'Steve Morris has written an inspirational, powerful and extraordinary book which is both universal in its appeal yet intimate in its impact upon individual souls.'

Jonathan Aitken

Lost
in
Wonder

**Glimpsing awe,
God
and the
good life**

Foreword by
Timothy Radcliffe OP

STEVE MORRIS

Authentic

27 26 25 24 23 22 21   7 6 5 4 3 2 1

First published 2021 by Authentic Media Limited,
PO Box 6326, Bletchley, Milton Keynes, MK1 9GG.
authenticmedia.co.uk

British Library Cataloguing in Publication Data
A catalogue record for this book is available from the British Library.
ISBN: 978-1-78893-150-2
978-1-78893-151-9 (e-book)

Some names and identifying details have been changed
to protect the privacy of individuals.

Cover design by Luke Porter
lukeporter.co.uk

Printed and bound by CPI Group (UK) Ltd, Croydon, CR0 4YY

COPYRIGHT
ACKNOWLEDGEMENTS

CONTENTS

CONTENTS

ACKNOWLEDGEMENTS

The author acknowledges, with thanks, permission to quote from his interviews and conversations with: Fr Timothy Radcliffe OP, Dr Michael Carter, Marian and Barry Sharp, Fr John of the Little Church Around the Corner, New York, Bishop Michael Colclough, the Revd Lyndon North, Pieter Laurens Mol and George Miles.

FOREWORD

Steve Morris brings all of his wide experience, profound faith and generosity of heart to his book on wonder. This is much to be welcomed since to wonder and be astonished is such a fundamental human experience. For many it is the door through which we come to a new perception of the world, seen as a radiant gift rather than mere stuff to be used and manipulated.

How does this happen? In moments of wonder when I am released from self-obsession, and liberated into a more spacious and gracious world. My earliest experiences of this came when I was a child. Often, I walked in the woods as dusk fell. I became intensely aware of the noises of animals, some settling down for the night and others waking and all of them keeping an eye on me. I was entering their world, a guest in their home. It was the thrilling experience of tiptoeing into a world filled with other ways of being alive as foxes, badgers, bats and owls and myriads of insects flourished in their own ways. Here I was not master.

Perhaps the most intense such experience was flying from Islamabad to Beijing over the Himalayas. The vast stillness of these probing peaks seemed majestic, almost divine. One could understand why, for some, they seemed like the home of the gods. How small and insignificant seemed my own worries and concerns as I flew over their vast stretch. How short was my stretch of life compared with the millennia during which these mountains came to be.

Sometimes this release from oneself comes with art or music. My father was a holy, kind, decent and truthful man who had a passion for music. He was quite shy and sometimes I found it hard to find the right words to say what I wanted. But once we listened to Allegri's 'Miserere' together and wept. We were transported beyond all shyness.

I was in Baghdad on 7 January 2015 when the offices of the Parisian satirical magazine, *Charlie Hebdo*, were attacked by terrorists. Twelve people were killed and eleven injured. The next day we travelled north to visit the refugee camps which sheltered people who had fled from the murderous attacks of ISIS on the towns and villages of the plain of Nineveh. I wondered what would be the atmosphere given that Christians and Muslims were camped in these places side by side. But everywhere I saw signs which proclaimed '*Je suis Charlie*'. People reached across boundaries, impelled by the horror of the moment. They were, even if only for a moment, drawn beyond old hostilities.

These experiences are ecstatic in the literal meaning of the world. One stands outside of oneself. One is brought beyond self-concern and even beyond old identities. This may lead one to an encounter with God. In the astonishing grace and givenness of the world, one senses the presence of the Alpha and Omega of all creation.

In the Acts of the Apostles there are at least two instances in which conversion is explicitly linked to this sort of ecstatic experience. In Acts 10, Peter sees a vision of animals, clean and unclean, lowered down from heaven. He is commanded to eat and at first refuses, but God commands him to do so since all food is made clean. This is described in the text as an experience of ecstasy. He transcends one of the markers of a separate Jewish identity, a boundary between the chosen people and the Gentiles. He comes to stand outside a previous self-understanding. It is as if at this moment he has an astonishing experience which remakes who he is. Also, we have the three accounts of the dramatic conversion of St Paul. His world is turned upside down and his identity is transformed.

Perhaps for most of us the journey of discipleship will involve some such transformative experience. We discover that we are not the centre of the world but brothers and sisters, children of the one Father. One of the most moving examples is that of the Timberline Cistercians, whose monastery in Algeria was caught up in the rising tide of violence in the 1990s. They debated whether to stay or go. Finally, they arrived at a consensus that they must stay, knowing that this would probably lead to their death.

Shortly before their murder in 1996, the Prior, Christian de Chergé, wrote his last will and testament in which he asserted that his life was given to these people.

Shortly after I visited the monastery recently, I was driven to the south of the country by a friend and fellow Dominican, Jean-Paul Vesco, the Bishop of Oran. We survived what could have been a very violent encounter with a mob and carried on to the north of the Sahara. We wanted to reach a small monastery but were not sure whether the route through the desert was viable. We stopped at an oasis and asked a local man who was with two of his sons. 'Not in that car,' he said. But we could see no other way and drove on. After a few miles the road disappeared into the desert. We turned around and saw that they had followed us. For a nervous moment I wondered if their motives were good. But when we met they said, 'We told you so. Come and stay with us.' For me this was a moment of ecstasy, of wonder. In the faces of these three Muslim men, I felt that I glimpsed the face of God. Their smile was God's. As in Genesis 18, there was the miracle of hospitality. The walls of division collapsed.

Fr Timothy Radcliffe OP

For Edward White, a man I never met.
Astronaut and pilgrim.

1

A Life with Wonder

What is wonder?

Wonder is elusive. We know what it is when we are in its presence, but it is hard to put into words. Sometimes it feels like an enchantment.

Of course, wonder takes us by surprise, or it wouldn't be wonder. It is that sense of sudden amazement when we see something beautiful, awesome, remarkable or just unfamiliar. We see something we thought was ordinary and realize that, instead, it is a thing of extraordinary complexity or power. Wonder shakes us from where we are and suddenly opens up a new vista.

There are many inflections to wonderment. Some describe it as a *feeling* of great surprise and joy, which is good because it explains why wonderment feels good and also like a gift. This is probably why there is such a temptation to chase after it and why that chase can also make us feel wistful or sad, as though without it we have lost part of our innocence, part of our awe. Wonderment is not part of the normal run of things, and we might feel strange in its presence. In Covid times, many of us have spent so much time indoors that our horizons have narrowed. We have just concentrated on taking one step at a time and getting through the day, and when we feel like this, life can lose a good deal of its colour.

Alister McGrath, in his book *Glimpsing the Face of God*,[1] argues that wonder is that which provokes a sense of longing and yearning. It is this yearning that drives us on to ask profound questions about the nature of creation, and to ask if God's fingerprints are all over the universe. The stars and the heavens perhaps expose the deep longing we have for God.

It is interesting that way back, before Jesus was born, there is an ancient prophecy in Isaiah that firmly pins wonderment and the Messiah together. The Messiah will be, we are told in Isaiah 9:6, the 'Wonderful Counsellor'. It is a lovely image, but one we are in danger of misunderstanding if we only look at it through a contemporary lens.

The actual meaning of wonder here is really something like 'incomprehensible'. Counsellor would have been understood as a profoundly wise king. Indeed, an incomprehensible counsellor seems like a figure ripe for humour. But in some ways, that's it. Jesus didn't make sense to people. People were confused by him. Wonder isn't about common sense, either. Wonder isn't about logic and straight lines – and that helps us to understand the very nonlinear Jesus, with his questions to answer questions and confusing parables.

Perhaps we have become way too prosaic, logical and even managerial in our churches. Carefully thought-through programmes, rotas and councils of elders are all useful to keep chaos at bay, but somewhere we need to find room for wonder. What if wonder is the real deal?

The best I can get to at this stage as I struggle to understand the odd power of wonder and wonderment is the story of a person that just about no one has heard of.

Edward White is my favourite astronaut.[2] He was the first American to do a space-walk. He was anarchic and playful. He was like a boy in a man's body. His space-walk was like ballet and he was dancing in the weightlessness. Despite the primitive equipment, he was lost in wonder and what could have just been a walk became a work of art, of poetry in motion.

He only had limited oxygen and his commander at mission control and his co-astronaut were begging him to come back in. But the wonder of it was too much and he had to be almost dragged in, nearly dead from lack of oxygen.

While he was out of the capsule he seemed joyous. He seemed to be almost out of his mind with the experience. This scandalized, or perhaps just worried, mission control. He was like a clownish child – lacking the gravitas of a later astronaut such as Neil Armstrong. He was like a bird set free.

The capsule eventually came down into the sea. When White was picked up, he was odd and distant. He didn't want to say anything about his experience of wonder to the media. Coming down to earth was painful and confronting.

Eventually he did speak.

He explained that when he had been a child, he used to go to Sunday school. He heard a lot about original sin but never understood it. He loved Bible stories, but they never seemed to really connect with him. But, he explained, after his experience of weightlessness and wonder in space he thought he had begun to understand what his Sunday school teachers were on about. Being earth-bound and not being able to fly, that was like original sin. What White wanted was to be able to fly, to lose the weight and baggage that he carried. We all do, don't we?

Maybe that's why I have become so interested in wonder. I want to be like Edward White. I sometimes think that Jesus' disciples might have felt a bit like Edward White – a sudden sense of weightlessness and new possibilities. As though they had stepped out of the prison of gravity and into something that felt like a dance more than a slog. Maybe they suddenly thought, 'Ah, this is what it is to fly, to be released from self and sin.'

But there is a sad coda to this story and it's the reason why you probably haven't heard of White. After his brush with wonder, he wanted to go back into space. Indeed, he was selected for an Apollo mission. But tragically an accident in the space capsule while training led to a fire, and White and his two fellow astronauts were killed.

He never got to go back into space. In some way, this book is in honour of this great American adventurer. A man I never knew, and who died while I was still a boy.

Find me some wonder

I want to find more wonder in my life and my faith. When I speak to other people – those of faith and those of none – they agree with me. They would like to find wonder as well. When we speak about it, we become aware of its elusive quality. But it is so easy to get into cycles in our lives that seem devoid of it.

The photographer and children's author Denys Watkins-Pitchford (1905–1990), known by the initials BB, loved nature. He used to have the following motto in each of his many books: 'The wonder of the world, the beauty and the power, the shapes of things, their colours, lights and shades, these I saw. Look ye also while life lasts.'[3] This little verse is so filled with the rumour of something wonderful at the heart of life on this tiny planet that we might do well to listen.

When I was a child, I experienced wonder more often than I have as an adult. Do we need to put 'the ways of childhood' behind us, as the apostle Paul suggests in 1 Corinthians 13:11? But if we do, does that scupper our chance of being full of wonder? Does it mean becoming all sensible – swapping play for numbers and rules and routines? Is it possible to be an adult and also have a world view of wonder?

St John, the gospel writer, referred to the followers of Jesus as 'children' (John 1:12,13) and Christ himself urged us to be more childlike. At the very least, the Bible whispers that we can, and perhaps should, rediscover something of our childish wonderment at the world and for God. What's more, that wonderment is no ephemeral thing. Instead, it might just be something that can help us to *see* and *be* differently; could it be one of the forgotten treasures of the old Christian Way? Perhaps the world is really filled with something that feels like magic.

I know that many of the times I feel wonder now, as a man in my fifties, it is associated with memory. I used to spend hours as a boy plane-spotting at Heathrow Airport. The place seemed impossibly glamorous to me. I imagined where those planes were travelling to and wondered about escaping the place I was growing up in. These days the merest smell of aircraft fuel, the smell of an airport, has me time-travelling back to my teenage years.

I find this intense sense of time-travel both mysterious and wonderful. But it also fills me with something that those who have written about the fleeting quality of wonder are familiar with. This remembrance of wonder-past fills me with a sense of longing and sadness.

If my hunch is right, the world is a far more mysterious, beautiful and amazing place than we give it credit for. If at the heart of this wonderment is a God of love who created it all, then we are going to have to seriously look at our world view.

At the beginning of his great mystical gospel, St John tells us that 'in the beginning was the Word'. It is a passage that has both enchanted and confused people. If he had substituted the Word for the name 'Jesus', it would have been much easier. But the meaning is clear. God has been here from the very start. If we get our theology straight about who that God is and what he is like, then we begin to be open to the possibility of wonder.

This book is a quest – I wanted to understand wonder better and to understand why I seem to have let it slip. I wanted to look for it (even if that is a fool's errand). I wanted, too, to be open to finding it wherever it is and to acknowledge that wonderment is a universal gift – not a command or a feeling reserved for the select few. But I am convinced that seeing God at the centre of wonderment gives us an even more profound understanding of how astounding things are.

I intend to turn over stones and see what I can find underneath. Where can we find wonder lurking? And can it be that wonder is more of a way of life than simply a disconnected feeling? If it is something more solid than just a feeling, then it opens up possibilities for the way we do life together, community together and church together.

To live the wonderful life will involve some risk, fresh thinking and perhaps even a little practise. But if it isn't something we grow out of, then it must be worth some time thinking how we might grow back into it again.

This morning, as I sit here typing, I can see the sun streaming through the trees. I can hear birds singing. My daughter is making tea in the kitchen. My little cats have settled themselves down on the settee for a good day's sleeping, and I am surrounded by people who have shown the kind of sacrificial love that you couldn't make up. I live in London, the greatest city in the world, and I can summon music into my space by simply speaking to a computer housed in a tiny plastic box. If I am lonely, I can even have a conversation with Alexa, my computer friend.

I might add to this that a short walk away is a hospital offering some of the highest-tech medicine known to humankind. I live in the borough of Brent, which is home to people from around the world, and we get on pretty well with each other. Oh, and I have the honour of being a priest and despite years of atheism, I am now a believer in God.

My father, Ralph, had the most difficult life. His father was killed in the war. He was bombed out during the Blitz. His grandfather moved in and beat him and made the family's life a misery. My father suffered from PTSD and depression. He had at least one breakdown. And finally, he developed that condition from hell – motor neurone disease. But he never saw that as the story of his life.

Just before he died, I was talking to him in the hospice. He had endured so much suffering. I was surprised when he said to me, 'Steve, I am so thankful; I have had a wonderful life.'

That statement amazed me and it amazes me still. What my father had figured out was that wonderment trumps despair. He felt wonderment because he had two sons, loved his wife, had done better for himself than he thought possible, enjoyed nature and friends, loved his country, had been proud to be a soldier, loved his mum and in the end, a few months before he died, he had come back to the God who had loved his dear Ralph all along.

Wonderment as the divine transaction

The rumour of wonderment runs alongside the rumour of God. In the book of Genesis, chapter 28, there is a telling description of how this wonderment might unfold.

Jacob, Isaac's son, has set off from home to look for a wife among his mother's family. He lies down to sleep in a nondescript place. An encounter with wonderment is probably the last thing on his mind. He dreams. His dream features God and a stairway to heaven. He sees angels going to-and-fro. In this dream, God makes him promises, to protect him, bless him and restore him. And Jacob finds new strength and purpose.

It is a beautiful picture of wonder because it contains so many of the elements we will look at later in this book. Wonder takes Jacob by surprise in a non-holy place. This seems to be a common occurrence for millions of people, both then and now. It shows that there is an odd transactional space between the wonder of heaven and the world itself. Wonder is a conversation between the

> Wonder is a conversation between the world we cannot quite see and the world that we can.

world we cannot quite see and the world that we can. Jesus straddles that divide – both man and God.

The impact is not so much religious as one full of wonder and surprise – God showed up, *here*! God who is outside of time and space also operates in time and space. If this is so, then we too can get a wild intimation that it might be possible to see behind the veil and fly like a bird set free.

To our modern preconceptions we might write this off as a psychological blip, a wish-fulfilment for a man under pressure. But it doesn't read that way. The experience of God and wonder seems oddly solid and real.

What Jacob does is to trust the experience he has and to let it count.

The bridge, the ladder between heaven and earth, may be just as open today as it was in the time of Jacob. Jesus promises it to his first followers. He says that they will see the transit between heaven and earth (John 1:51).

I want intimations of this divine transaction – I want to know how this wonder might translate into my own life and the life of my family, community and church.

This is where I start my quest. I wonder where you are starting yours from?

Study Questions

Wonder is elusive. We know what it is when we are in its presence, but it is hard to put into words. Sometimes it feels like an enchantment.

Do you agree? How does wonder feel to you?

I want to find more wonder in my life and my faith. When I speak to other people – those of faith and those of none – they agree with me. They would like to find wonder as well.

How do you experience a sense of wonder in your faith? Do you share the sense of wanting more wonderment? Why? Or why not?

The impact is not so much religious as one full of wonder and surprise – God showed up, here! *God who is outside of time and space also operates in time and space. If this is so, then we too can get a wild intimation that it might be possible to see behind the veil and fly like a bird set free.*

Discuss.

Prayer

Father, help us to experience more wonderment in our faith and in our life. Open us up to the amazing world around us and to the experience of peace and enquiry that comes along with wonder. Help us to be surprised by wonder and to understand more of what it is and where it comes from.
If we are feeling lonely or worn down, help us to see beyond the day-to-day troubles we have. Let us have something of the spirit of the astronauts and the wonderment they felt and carried with them throughout their lives.

2

The Amazement of Liminal Places and Events

Towards the beginning of Luke's Gospel (5:17–25), Jesus is teaching. It must have been daunting because his opponents the Pharisees have come to watch and presumably aim to trip him up. People have come from everywhere. Jesus breaks off the teaching because he is suddenly full of the kind of wondrous power that allows him to heal people.

At this point some men appear who have with them their friend who is paralysed. In a way, this is where the wonder begins because it is the wonder of sacrificial friendship. They love their friend and they refuse to believe the evidence of their own eyes. Logic says that their friend is paralysed and will stay this way. But they have a wild hope and they love their friend enough to carry him across town.

Indeed, so keen are they to get their friend to Jesus that they make a hole in the roof of the house where Jesus is teaching and lower him down. It has an edge of comedy, surely. After a discussion about the nature of sin and forgiveness, the man is healed.

You might think that the healing is the source of wonderment in this passage. But I am not so sure. I find it wondrous that the Christ does something that is so kindly. But it is what happens next that is perhaps the most wondrous.

Christ sends the healed man home – to his family and friends. He doesn't demand he come on the road with him, make any commitment to following him or anything. He just tenderly sends him home. He sends him back to his everyday life, but with a new wonderment in his heart. It is an affirmation of the importance of homelife and of carrying on as normal. He allows him to go on with his life, but that life is now infused with wonderment. It is perhaps no surprise that:

Everyone was amazed and gave praise to God. They were filled with awe and said, 'We have seen remarkable things today.'

Luke 5:26

It only takes a brush with mortality for ourselves or someone we love to be profoundly grateful that we, or they, are still here. Life is precious. Every ordinary life is extraordinary when seen close up, and that is truly wonderful.

If we can rediscover wonder, then perhaps the faith will be of such winning proportions that anyone would seem daft not to sign up. 'Revival' is just another word for when those who had lost hope begin to feel wonder again and see life afresh in all its holiness, beauty and creativity. It is the kind of thing that transformed the fearing and lost community on the Day of Pentecost and birthed the Christian church. If church and Christian community was to become a place of wonder (as opposed simply to wonders), who could resist being part of it?

Ah, but we must be careful. 'Signs and wonders' (Rom. 15:19) can be misused – but wonder is far bigger than these.

Wonder is out there and people of all faiths and none have listened to the hints it gives that life is more than something we can touch and feel. Catch a sunset or a sunrise, hear the sound of the garden birds, experience an unexpected touch of compassion from a friend, or read about the lives of the old saints and we begin to feel that life may be more magical than we ever imagined.

In an age of fake news and mistrust of big narratives, the idea that there is a God-given and inspired sense of almost childish wonder available is a revolutionary thought. We moderns are yearning for wonder, and are full of curiosity about where it might come from, and how we might have more of it. Perhaps we tend to search for it in the wrong places. The wonders of technology, for instance, offer much that is amazing, but they cannot really be there when we need lifting out of ourselves – they cannot be a sunny day or a parent's love.

Holman Hunt's famous painting *The Light of the World* shows Christ about to knock on an overgrown and long unopened door. I sometimes think that overgrown doorway is a metaphor for the opening of our spiritual and religious life to the power and beauty of God in all its awesome and wonderful power.

During the life of Jesus, his followers sometimes felt the kind of doorway pictured in *The Light of the World* swing open.

The historian speaks

When we begin to open that door to wonder, we begin to see it everywhere.

At the time of writing, Dr Michael Carter is senior historian at English Heritage. I interviewed him, as something of an after-thought, for an article I was writing for *The Spectator* on the

When we begin to open that door to wonder, we begin to see it everywhere.

new museum at Whitby Abbey. Michael told me that he wasn't a person of 'religious observance'. But as we spoke, we got well beyond the retelling of history and into the great question of wonderment. It turns out that his love of history isn't just about telling a narrative; it is about sharing something much deeper.

When I spoke to Michael, I had a question about the museum at the old ruined abbey that wouldn't let me go – how on earth could a museum capture the elusive quality of such a place of signs and wonders? To be honest, I was wondering about writing an article that was vaguely critical of the whole enterprise of building a museum, and gift shop. But Michael's story won me over so powerfully that I felt it had to be told.

Michael told me:

> Whitby is breathtaking and it has this huge emo-
> tional and spiritual impact. When I was a child, I
> used to visit the great old ruined northern mon-
> asteries with my parents. I found them places of
> wonder; they stirred my soul.

This sense of amazement just grew for young
Michael. He began reading about the lives of the
old saints and the regular people who lived in these
ancient sites. The insight he gained into their lives
and struggles, their emotions and beliefs, again gave
him a great sense of wonder.

> I decided to become a historian, because I wanted
> people to be as moved and excited as I was. The
> wonder and the mystery got hold of me – it does
> to thousands of others who come here. I realized
> that this sense of amazement speaks directly to
> twentieth-century people.
>
> At the core of these old sites, these monasteries,
> is something that speaks to our human needs –
> we just needed to find a way of discussing this.[1]

This non-faith modern historian had somehow fallen
in love with the strange power of wonderment. It
is no coincidence that he did so in places that are

steeped in prayer. These 'thin' places can be places where we feel God very closely.

Wonder and shallow evangelism

It would be insulting and plain untrue to say that a sense of wonder is reserved for followers of Christ. Wonder is universal, and people of all faiths and none have access to it. But is wonder sharpened and made even deeper when we see what or who lies behind it?

We must avoid being smug. I wonder, is there any truth in the assertion that Christians have sometimes forgotten wonder while in the grip of shallow evange-lism and the onslaught of health and wealth preach-ing? When we simply repeat that God has a plan for us in the most micro-detail, we have to ask ourselves important questions. Is it possible to find any won-der when a loved one is diagnosed with dementia, our children drop out of university, or we find our-selves going bankrupt? Was that in God's plan? If so, he would seem a strange friend indeed. Is there any wonderment to be had in these wilderness places? Wonder can be a slippery character. It can take us unaware and be found in places we least expect it.

We need a world view that can deal with the harsh realities of life and still find wonderment. At its most basic, as I once heard it said, perhaps it is as simple as waking up in the morning and realizing that we are still alive and have another chance at life in the day ahead.

When we are at the end of ourselves and we feel depressed, anxious or despairing, wonder can seem in short supply. However, Jesus never promises a trouble-free life; in fact, quite the opposite. But in our world, one that is infected with deep consumerism, how can we express and feel wonder if we don't live up to the dream that we can spend and buy our way out of unhappiness?

We might distinguish between *markers* of wonder and the *living* of a life that has wonder at its daily core. Wonder is not amazement that we have done so well, or been so clever, or anything like that. It is that God has chosen to love people, despite all the reasons he might choose not to. And the word for that is 'grace'.

It is grace that really powers our sense of wonder, but there are other things too. It is amazing that we are capable of understanding something of the way that the universe works. It is amazing that there are laws in science that we can use to explain something of the wonder of the world. It is amazing that we have the ability to know that we are alive and to be cognisant.

I wonder about wonder

Sometimes I wonder about wonder. What kind of power does it have and can we even trust it?

The world was touched by Prince Harry's words on the birth of his first son, Archie.[2] He spoke about it as a kind of wonder – an amazing experience. And he felt wonder at his wife and what she had done. It moved beyond the trite to a real appreciation of what it takes to give birth and the beautiful role of women – not just in childbirth, but more generally. The newspapers carried the story and reflected that this might be the start of a real kind of transforming feminism – one that starts with wonder as well as rights and obligations.

But how long can this sense last? Many men are full of wonder at their partners and the amazing courage it takes to give birth. And yet. Men continue to abuse women, pay them less than they deserve and demean them. If wonder is just a passing moment – a fleeting glimpse at something special – then we can ignore its call to us to live differently.

The same goes for our planet. Few have escaped its wondrous power. A glorious sunrise, a mountain range, the songs of the birds can lift us out of the everyday. We are struck by how amazing the place we call home is. And yet. We treat our planet with contempt – polluting it and destroying species. We may enjoy seeing the natural world as it is portrayed in a TV show, but can this have the power to have any impact on the way we actually behave?

Jesus had the same kind of experience. His miracles caused wonder – of course they did. But they were not enough in themselves. Even having seen a miracle, people often shrugged their shoulders and carried on as normal. People did not always come back to thank him.[3] In the case of his last miracle – raising Lazarus from the dead[4] – it probably created a certain amount of bemusement rather than lasting spiritual revolution. Although there was clearly thankfulness from the family, real concern from the authorities, and a surge of belief – see John 12:1– 10 – it still wasn't enough. In the end Jesus had to be the miracle. He had to put his own life down in order to change things.

Early days of wonder

It is tempting to look at the wondrous life, death and resurrection of Jesus and to stop there. But there is an intriguing passage in the book of Acts (Acts 3:1– 10) that points to the currency of wonder – what it feels like. Peter and John are walking towards the temple. It is just an ordinary day. They meet a man who has been disabled from birth. Each day he is carried to one of the temple gates where he joins the other beggars.

It is hard to envisage what a dispiriting life it must have been. Sitting each day, begging, isn't exactly a life outcome most people would want for themselves. The beggar asks Peter and John for money – he sees them as meal tickets.

They explain that they have no money but have something even more precious for him. They heal the man in the name of Jesus. His ordinary day, and theirs, has become a thing of wonderment. Unsurprisingly, the beggar leaps for joy. But the reaction of the crowd is even more impressive. They recognize the threadbare old beggar and see him leaping around and praising God. They were 'filled with wonder and amazement' (Acts 3:10).

Amazement and wonder are siblings. We don't get one without the other. Wonder is powerful and calls us to be amazed – which sometimes feels like a tall order.

Study Questions

It only takes a brush with mortality for ourselves or someone we love to be profoundly grateful that we, or they, are still here.

Discuss.

'Whitby is breathtaking and it has this huge emotional and spiritual impact. When I was a child, I used to visit the great old ruined northern monasteries with my parents. I found them places of wonder; they stirred my soul.'

What places have stirred your soul and why?

Sometimes I wonder about wonder. What kind of power does it have and can we even trust it?

What do you think?

Prayer

*Father, I want to experience wonder and break free
from some of the confines of my life. Sometimes
I know that wonder is out there and deep within
me as well, but I forget to pay attention to it, and
get on with a life focused on myself. Remind me of
some of the times I have experienced wonder and
felt you close to me. Make these moments real
to me and help me to gain courage and strength
from them.*

*I know that there is wonder in the world and that
you are the source of this. Would you help me to
open my eyes to wonderment and not to look for it
in the wrong place?*

*Help us to be amazed by you and for that
amazement to be fresh every day. Help us to
look at the people around us and see something
of your love, creativity and joy in them. When I
wonder about wonder, help me to see the wood for
the trees.*

3

Close to Home

We live on a ball of rock in a galaxy of billions of stars and planets. Our planet is moving at 67,000 miles an hour, and yet we have no sense of this mind-boggling speed, otherwise we would be hanging on for grim death. We travel many thousands of miles a day but never know it. We experience a settled world and we get used to so many things that, when really thought about, are quite amazing.

It has taken scientists and TV programmes to help us to see how extraordinary it is simply to be alive.

Seen from space, our world is an illuminated water-world like a jewel in the infinite darkness. The world is impossibly beautiful. And if we truly are the only planet containing life, then we really are precious beyond our wildest dreams. If we are alone, then we are the best on offer and our world is the ultimate in creation.

It is telling that the astronauts so frequently report, not so much on the wonder of space, but on the wonder of looking back upon our home planet.

A new way of life

If wonder is the key to a new way of life, we had better take it seriously. To be a person of wonder is surely to open ourselves to not being logical, to open ourselves to being regularly astonished and to recapture something of childlike innocence. It is, of course, countercultural in a world that tells us to toughen up and grow up.

Hollywood understands wonder – it has a narrative about it. Take a film like Tom Hanks' 1988 hit *Big*.[1] In it a boy called Josh Baskin visits one of those fortune-telling attractions at an old fairground. He's 12 years old. He wishes that he was big and suddenly finds himself a child in a man's body.

It is a poignant film. At its core is a disconnect. When he becomes big he retains his wonder and this makes him a unique adult – childlike, brilliant and vulnerable. He becomes the vice-president of a toy company; of course, he understands toys in a way no adult can. But the child in the man isn't happy, and after an adventure, he finds the old Zoltar machine again and goes back to childhood.

On the one hand it is a study of wonder. But it also shows the limit of Hollywood's imagination. Wonder only works when a child becomes a man. But what if men and women didn't need to time-travel back to childhood to be wondrous again? What if we adults could be both adult and full of wonderment?

Seeing things differently

In literary theory there is a concept that can help us to see things differently. Great literature tends to be part of an act of *defamiliarization*. When we read a novel of power and beauty, we see what seemed a common thing or experience in a different or strange way. In turn, this changes our whole perception of what is familiar. We see things afresh.

Defamiliarization helps us to be childlike. The first time we, for instance, encountered an escalator, it seemed a thing of total brilliance and an opportunity for great fun. When we grow up it is just a way of going up a floor or two and is less tiring than using the stairs.

Jesus actually used this very technique in his parables and sayings. The camel passing through the eye of a needle (Matt. 19:24) is a prime case of taking a familiar thing and, cartoon-like, defamiliarizing it. The aim is to make things strange and wonderful. It is a technique that keeps us listening and tends to overcome our defences when we have set our hearts in stone. We understand Christ's teaching a lot more if we see the way he uses defamiliarization. Interestingly, it is the same technique that comedians often use. In the hands of a comedian, what seems like something quite normal can be twisted and shaped into something fantastical, sinister, or outrageous.

We see a great example of this in the story of St Paul as told in Acts 9. Paul is going about his business as usual. He is a clever man, one of the cleverest of his generation, and he has a purpose in life, which is to persecute the new Christian sect. He is that dangerous combination of intelligence, vehemence and violence. We see people like that these days and they create mayhem too. Nothing is new.

Paul is given a mission to round up some Christians and bring them back to Jerusalem for possible torture and death. He is a feared man and one can only imagine the agitation felt by the early followers of the Way. They know the violence that he is capable of and have probably heard of the awful tortures that have gone on. No one would have been spared and the sense of terror would have been obvious.

And then something happens that changes the contours of his ordinary day – an event of terror and wonder. (It is interesting how the two often seem to go together.)

As Paul nears the great city of Damascus, a blinding light shines from heaven. It flashes around Paul. One can only imagine how light that light must have been. But God isn't finished with the wayward executioner yet. Paul falls to the ground and then he hears the audible voice of Jesus. And Jesus is calling him by name and asking him the agonizing question, 'why do you persecute me?' (v. 4). This is followed by an instruction to go to the city to receive a further message.

When Paul gets to his feet, he realizes that he cannot see. This once arrogant man has to be led by the hand and then has to wait a further three days, blind and helpless, for the next stage in his journey. Paul must have been terrified. For the powerful to suddenly feel helpless is a very sobering experience.

One remembers Saddam Hussein being found in a hole when his regime fell. The pomp and power had gone, and what remained was a very shrunken figure. Perhaps Paul was in the same kind of place and suffering the same kind of diminution.

A follower of Jesus, Ananias, is sent to get Paul. Ananias was brave – he must have feared for his life. No Christian would voluntarily meet up with such a dangerous enemy. But Ananias was emboldened by God. He lays hands on Paul and he can see again. Ananias, who would have been one of the Christians Paul was rounding up, calls Paul 'brother' and explains Jesus wants him to be filled with the Holy Spirit (v. 17). Ananias is a man filled with grace and his work is one of awe and wonder.

As Paul opens his eyes and can see, I am sure that Ananias, the man who laid his human hands on Paul, is filled with such wonder at God's forgiveness and power that he would have been speaking about it for the rest of his life.

Paul's life has been totally transformed by this wonderful, fearsome event. In fact, what has happened is a change in perception. Paul will have to deal with an inconvenient fact. All the rules and regulations of his Jewish faith are no way of getting closer to God. In fact, life and salvation is unnervingly much simpler than he thought. His legalism couldn't survive.

And he realizes something – Jesus is God. It is a real-ization of such wonder that he has no option than to start his life over again, with different priorities and a different world view.

This sense of wonderment that the ultimate being might humble himself to help us to be free, pow-ered the early disciples and has continued to strike a deep chord with millions of others over the centu-ries. The sheer numbers seem to argue against this being a mass fantasy. God refuses to die out.

We are told that 'something like scales fell from [Paul's] eyes' (v. 18) and he is baptized on the spot. His life is about to take a turn towards suffering and many hard miles on the road – but his wonderment in what happened to him never leaves him.

Wonderment sometimes comes with an imperative that life cannot be the same again. When we deal with the wonder of God, it isn't simply an entertainment or a nice holy experience, it is a call to a new way of life. The word we use for this kind of wonder is 'conversion'.

Wonder outside the worship service

Sometimes a worship service can leave us flat. If we feel that we aren't finding wonder in a worship ser-vice, then perhaps we need to take a step elsewhere and see what we find. Where do most of us feel wonder?

The birth of a child, especially if you happen to be there, is a thing of wonder. My mother told me that when they took me home from hospital after I had been born, they took me wrapped in a blanket to their best friends' house. My mother knocked on their friends' door, and as they opened it, my father said, 'Look what we've made.'

Another great source of wonder is the extraordinary business of human ingenuity and creation. In our mid-twenties my wife, Christine, and I went to New York. We'd never been before and were strangely ignorant of what to expect.

We were on a budget, so we took one of the min-ibuses that run from John F. Kennedy International Airport. Anyone who has taken this journey knows that, for some time, it is a nondescript route through the suburbs with just hints of Manhattan Island on the horizon.

It was dark and we were just able to see the streets that lay immediately either side of the road. After some time we drove onto the Queensboro Bridge. It is a Gothic structure and is striking on its own merits – it sums up a New York feeling. It was then that my wife tapped me on the shoulder. Out of the window, there was Manhattan – millions of lights and tower blocks forming grand canyons of human design.

I have rarely had the experience of my mouth dropping open in wonder, but there it was. Manhattan at night rendered us speechless. There is something of great beauty here, and the signifiers of American life – the signs, the yellow cabs and those air vents – all lead to a sense that this is just how this great city should be.

The others in the bus were as awestruck as us. Our desire, I am sure, was to watch and wonder and be ready to get out and explore and experience what was here.

Perhaps the other main way we discover wonder is through the amazing natural world around us.

Sometimes on a dark night, looking at the moon, I am aware that I am just one creature among a billion living in a darkened galaxy looking at a piece of space rock. I feel more like an astronaut then than a vicar. Or maybe it might be better to say I feel like the boy I was when I watched men land on the moon and wondered if, one day, I might travel up there too. I had no idea of the odds a boy from a regular school, whose father was a carpet fitter, might face to go into space. But that didn't matter, a new possibility had come onto my horizon and I joined a whole generation who wished that one day they might take a step into the deep unknown.

But now I know that you don't have to go into space to find wonder. It is much closer to home.

Study Questions

On the one hand [Big] is a study of wonder. But it also shows the limit of Hollywood's imagination. Wonder only works when a child becomes a man. But what if men and women didn't need to time-travel back to childhood to be wondrous again? What if we adults could be both adult and full of wonderment?

What do you make of this comment on the way Hollywood sees and portrays wonder? What are the strengths and weaknesses of the Hollywood approach?

Wonderment sometimes comes with an imperative that life cannot be the same again. When we deal with the wonder of God, it isn't simply an entertainment or a nice holy experience, it is a call to a new way of life. The word we use for this kind of wonder is 'conversion'.

Discuss.

Sometimes a worship service can leave us flat. If we feel that we aren't finding wonder in a worship service, then perhaps we need to take a step elsewhere and see what we find. Where do most of us feel wonder?

Has worship ever left you feeling flat? Where might you look elsewhere for wonderment?

Prayer

Thank you for those moments of grace that we feel. When all seems against us, we are aware of an odd knowledge of your love. Please comfort us – whisper words of comfort and love.

We wonder how Paul must have felt when his life became darkness and then he got that second chance to see again. We pray the kind of prayer of wonder he must have prayed – but wonderment with uncertainty about what it all means. Can we be brave enough to take a risk on wonderment? What will we need to see differently and do differently?

What is wonderment whispering to us, our families and our communities?

Jesus, we place ourselves in your hands, ready to be amazed – amazed by things big or small, close or far.

4

The Dance of Wonder

Marian and Barry began coming to our weekly memory café. They arrive in a large, specially adapted van that their son, Paul, travels in with them. He has severe cerebral palsy and cannot speak, but has full control of his motorized wheelchair. We hear Marian as she comes into the church to say a hello, and this is followed by her family who tumble in afterwards.

Over the weeks, I began to spend a lot of time talking to Marian and Barry. They told me how Paul is their pride and joy and how much they love him. It was easy to see why. Seeing that bond between parent and son was very moving indeed. It has certainly helped me to see the person and the people and not the situation.

In a society that has, to say the least, questionable attitudes towards those with disabilities, it was wonderful. The temptation is to see Paul's disability as a tragedy and his effect on his parents as a lifelong burden. The emphasis is on the 'dis' of disability. But this isn't at all the picture we get from Paul and his family.

If they missed a week, we felt we were missing something. Paul was becoming our pride and joy as well. The place felt odd without them. We somehow lost a bit of the DNA of our café if we didn't have Paul and co. with us. And that wasn't just because of the delicious home-made cake Marian always brings.

After a while, Paul and his parents began to come on a Sunday to church. We'd hear the van pull up and then scurry out to get the ramp set up for church so Paul could get in. They became part of the Sunday family here.

Each month, before the coronavirus outbreak of 2020, we did café church on a Sunday. We invited people to bring their dogs. We served a magnificent breakfast, and we tended to have a time of discussion during the service. It was our best-attended service of the month and something we all looked forward to.

For some reason, on one café church Sunday I was feeling low. It had been a tough week and I felt a huge responsibility for the service. It was a classic case of trying to do things in my own strength. Before the service I was shaking with nerves and wondering if I was suited at all to being a vicar.

Above all, my faith felt like it had run thin and cold. It is a thing many other ministers have felt brave enough to admit to. Sometimes standing up there is the loneliest place in the world. When faith is at a low ebb, all we can do is carry on and hang on and say whatever prayers we can muster and pray with those around us.

Before the service I told my vergers how I was feeling. They sat me down and laid hands on my shoulders and prayed a gentle prayer. I think it involved me relaxing and the Holy Spirit filling me with faith and joy (and wonder) again. The main thing was I had made known where I was at and that was a good thing.

As we began, I was feeling a little better, but still a bit flat. I was no longer shaking. We moved into worship and our band began.

As I looked back into the congregation, I noticed that a circle had formed. In the centre of the circle was Paul, spinning wildly in his chair. His mum and dad were looking on in a kind of wonder, full of love. Paul was leading us in a dance of faith. His wheelchair was no impediment – in fact it was an advantage. It span perfectly in a circle. Round and round.

Paul danced because he could. We followed because we wanted to. Afterwards, someone said to me that Paul dancing and coming to church was a living symbol of what we had become as a church. They told me that church did not feel like a club – it felt like a family, with all the glorious messiness that that entails.

Later, as Paul and his parents came up for communion, I leaned forward to place the wafer in Paul's mouth.

'Careful!' his mum said to me. 'He bites.'

She broke out into a smile. It was a joke. Paul doesn't bite. Either literally or metaphorically.

At the end of the service, I thanked Paul and his parents and said how much his wondrous dance meant to us and to God. I simply let my own tattered faith be transported by his freedom and joy. I began the service flat – a kind of shell going through the motions. I ended it full of conviction that wonder is at the heart of everything. It took a young man with cerebral palsy and his dance of amazement to shock me out of my introspection.

Perhaps that is one of the functions of wonder – of why it is a medicine that we could take more often. Wonder is a way of getting over ourselves and seeing the true pattern of the universe. That true pattern

> Wonder is a way of getting over ourselves and seeing the true pattern of the universe.

is us, in all our own disablement, dancing still, just because we can.

Marian fished out a piece of paper from her pocket. 'Steve, we have something we wrote for Paul. He loves to hear it. We read it with him every day. It is based on Psalm 23. Would you like to read it?'

This is their poem of wonder and joy and affirmation that life is wonderful, and so it is.

> The Lord helps me in my electric wheelchair
> He makes me comfortable in my seat.
> He gives me knowledge of what to do.
> He knows I can't sing so he taught me how to dance.
> Where other people sing to praise God, I dance.

The Lord will always know the turn of my wheels and the beat of my heart will be in perfect harmony to any song.

God knows my every thought and everything about me.

He guides me along all roads even though some appear

Hard and hilly, the Lord is always with me.

He prepares a table before me to refresh me.

He oils my wheelchair parts and my speed improves.

Good times and safe journeys will be with me always.

Then after, I will dwell in the house of the Lord forever.[1]

As I am about to talk to someone else, Marian tugs at my shirt-sleeve:

When we had Paul, we knew nothing at all about disability. We didn't know what to expect. But having Paul has fulfilled us – he has fulfilled us. He has given us more than we have ever given him.

Study Questions

The Lord helps me in my electric wheelchair
He makes me comfortable in my seat.
He gives me knowledge of what to do.
He knows I can't sing so he taught me how to dance.
Where other people sing to praise God, I dance.

Discuss. How does this impact on you? Does it help you to think of wonder in a new way? Do you have examples of this kind of wonder in your own life and family?

Prayer

Open our eyes to the wonderment in the lives of others. Help us to see how you are working through them – helping us to dance the eternal dance. Paul has an impairment we can see, but ours are sometimes hidden from others.

Help us to see ourselves as you see us and be honest with each other in areas where we struggle. Help us to be open to joy, whatever the circumstances we find ourselves in.

Let us be led into wonderment by our friends and family and brothers and sisters in the faith. Turn our wheels to the beat of our heart so we can join in the eternal song of praise and wonder. 'Holy, holy, holy is the LORD Almighty'.[2]

In all our brokenness let wonder be the call of our hearts. Help us to spread it around and share it with others.

5

The Farmer and the Donkey

I once stayed near a farm on holiday.[1] They keep a herd of rare-breed cows with magnificent horns and shaggy coats. I liked to take a stroll over to the farm and say hello to my donkey friend that lived in the field right beside the busy road. Henry was a lovely chap and was partial to having his ear stroked. I always felt better having spent some time with the donkey. I think we formed a kind of friendship; I had certainly hoped so.

The farmer told me that until a few years ago Henry shared his paddock with a friend – another male, called Danny. The two followed each other round and were rarely more than a few feet apart. They were inseparable and never seemed to have disagreements – although, of course, we are not really aware of what a donkey disagreement looks like. Although perhaps it involves braying and the odd bite.

One day, when the farmer went to the stable where the donkeys slept, he found that Danny had died during the night. For all that night and for the coming day, Henry stood watch over his fallen friend. Occasionally he would nuzzle his old comrade, but most of the time he just stood by him in that calm, stoical donkey way.

The farmer told me that when a donkey's soulmate dies, you should not separate them at once. You have to leave them for at least twenty-four hours so the surviving donkey can say goodbye. If you don't, it causes huge angst for the surviving donkey. The farmer told me that they have to be left to mourn because they need that time to say their goodbyes.

This is not anthropomorphism or wishful thinking. For those of us who share our homes and lives with pets, it opens up a vista onto the creativity of God and the truth that love truly is the currency that makes the most sense of things.

> Love truly is the currency that makes the most sense of things.

When I went back the next year, Henry, too, died. I felt like I should have stood sentinel with his body as he prepared to be welcomed into the loving arms of his maker. I would gladly have marked the life of this fine animal. After all, Jesus had a thing for donkeys and trusted them to be his executive transport when he didn't have access to a grand Roman chariot or a posh horse. And indeed, we are even treated to a talking donkey in the Old Testament (Num. 22:21–33).

But the farmer's story about his old donkeys says something of the mystery and beauty of the animals we spend our lives with. Perhaps it should also cause us to wonder if we might be much kinder to them and appreciative of them. I have often thought that when we go to heaven, Jesus will ask us why we didn't appreciate more the animals we shared our lives with.

Where does Jesus lead us?

It might help if we had more evidence of Jesus and his followers' care for pets and other animals. If we heard the story of the day Jesus stopped to pick up an abandoned kitten, or stroke a dog, it would help. If we had a parable about the lonely donkey, it would give us a clue. If St Paul had a faithful pet dog that accompanied him on his journeys and brought him some joy amid the slog that he underwent, then we might not just think better of him, we might appreciate the wonder of our animal friends. I wish we had more evidence of animals, especially in the New Testament.

We don't have much evidence for the keeping of pets. Part of this is probably down to the cultural context in which Jesus' life and ministry are set. Although, at one point, we do hear that there were dogs under the tables (Mark 7:28). But we do get clues about the importance of creatures.

The parable of the lost sheep in Luke 15 isn't simply a metaphor for the lostness of humans. It is about real sheep and the fact that they are precious – so precious that a shepherd would risk his life to save a single one of them. If it wasn't about the reality of the animals we share our world with, it would have had no real connection with Jesus' listeners – people who understood that the crucial interrelatedness of livestock and family was much more than simply financial. The people knew that keeping their livestock in reasonable health would have a bearing on the family's wellbeing.

Animals that do get a bit of coverage are birds, and among them are sparrows. These delightful little birds were allowed to build their nests in the temple. Jesus' sayings point to how important even this little bird is to God.

Jesus says, 'Look at the birds of the air; they do not sow or reap or store away in barns, and yet your heavenly Father feeds them. Are you not much more valuable than they?' (Matt. 6:26). And later on, in 10:29, Jesus says: 'Are not two sparrows sold for a penny? Yet not one of them will fall to the ground outside your Father's care.'

I think we can at least say that God has his eye on the world around us. God cares about the little birds. They are precious to him and their lives matter.

In fact, I have a story about the way a little bird built up my faith. Many Christians attend a Walk of Witness event on Good Friday. I have to confess that I greatly dislike these events. Why? Long before I was a Christian, I was an atheist/agnostic. The only time I came across Christians publicly was when I was stuck behind a small troop of miserable people, walking in silence, behind a person holding a cross.

For me it was the worst possible advert for the faith. I had enough misery in my life without joining this miserable bunch, at least that's what I thought then.

Sadly, my view hasn't really changed that much. I find the WoW a really grim affair. I know that it's probably not meant to be a time of clowns and trumpets and singing and dancing. One year I felt particularly unhappy on the march as we fought our way along the streets in Brent, pursued by car drivers hooting their horns and people looking at us, bemused. I know I am a parish priest and I should have just put up with it. But I found myself getting really hot under the collar.

About three-quarters of the way round I hopped on a bus and came back to my vicarage. Needless to say, I was full of guilt and thinking what a useless priest I was. It is hard to describe just how guilty we sometimes feel when we don't live up to our ideal of the ordained life. Incidentally, one of the advantages of reading the lives of the saints is that we find people there who are only too human and fragile. When we get into the detail it is, perhaps, surprising that they aren't paragons of virtue. They are like the rest of us – grumpy, unreasonable and all the other things we live down to.

Anyway, back at the vicarage it was at least a beautiful day. The sky was the deepest blue, the garden had been recently tidied up and the flowers were coming though. There is a beautiful and very old oak tree in our garden which looks different depending on what time of year it is and how the light catches it.

Sitting in my garden with a cup of coffee I was a bit shell-shocked. Why had my reaction been so violent – even disproportionate? I sometimes disappoint myself. Sitting in the gloomy churches along the route and walking in morbid silence had made me totally miserable and not in a good way – by which I mean a kind of sombre, serious 'reflecting on life' sort of way. It was then that a little friend hopped over to me. Our garden robin had made it all the way back from his winter in Spain or Portugal and he was back with us in our garden in Brent.

This bonny little bird wasn't in a hurry. Indeed, he came over to have a look at me before heading back to his favourite bush. For the next half an hour I watched the beautiful little creature with true wonder. I was struck by his beautiful red breast and his delicate movements. I wonder what he was thinking about me.

I was in a place where I could take the medicine I needed.

The animals that we share our planet with have a kind of grace about them. In their behaviour and calm we see something that we ourselves are sometimes short of. Animals don't seem to worry themselves about much. They don't look into the future and predict disaster. They simply are. In this there is an odd echo of the way God describes himself. He is 'I AM', he tells us in Exodus 3:14. This implies that he is more about being than doing, just as animals are, and that is a wondrous thought indeed. It is also a caution to us activists who are so intent on doing things that we miss something wonderful in going slowly, taking our time and doing not so much.

At 12 o'clock, I was back in the church ready to run a service of 'The Hour at the Cross' and felt restored.

Our sacred house guests

The nearest we get to the wonder of pets in the first millennium of the church is the Celtic saints who had a veritable menagerie of animal friends and companions. But these days we have God's creatures closer to hand, and if we are honest, and take time to think about it, we might see some of his glory in our animal house guests.

I share my house with three cats and in my friendship with them I feel that I've seen much that has not just filled me with wonder, but also allowed me to see the glory of God. If you have a pet, I am sure you find in them an acceptance and appreciation that causes you to wonder, too. Whether it is a cat, a dog, a rabbit, a bird, we can learn so much from the way they are; their fun, their enjoyment of life, their trusting natures – their attachment to us, and their love. In a sense, they are our sacred house guests, sharing our day-to-day lives.

We often wonder if our pets will be in heaven. The truth is, I don't know. But it wouldn't be heaven without them, would it?

Study Questions

Jesus says, 'Look at the birds of the air; they do not sow or reap or store away in barns, and yet your heavenly Father feeds them. Are you not much more valuable than they?' (Matt. 6:26). And later on, in 10:29, Jesus says: 'Are not two sparrows sold for a penny? Yet not one of them will fall to the ground outside your Father's care.'

How do you respond to these words? What does it mean to you that God cares for animals, and how might it change the way you think about them? How might it change the way we behave towards animals?

But these days we have God's creatures closer to hand, and if we are honest, and take time to think about it, we might see some of his glory in our animal house guests.

Discuss.

Prayer

Thank you for the animals that we share our homes with – our cats and dogs and rabbits and birds. Help us to see them as a blessing and wonderment, and to care for them well as honoured guests and friends. Help us to grow in wonderment and respect for animals.
Let us be open to learning from our pets and animal friends. Let us experience wonder at their stillness and trusting natures and perception and beauty. Help us to appreciate their simple love for us and to see their grace and enthusiasm for life.
Help us to fight for justice towards all living creatures and to fight cruelty towards animals wherever we encounter it.

6

A Trip to Southwark

The big challenge was not to lose any of the sixty-five very frail and elderly people we were transporting to Southwark Cathedral. It didn't help that the organisers had provided a school bus for us and we were cramped. As the doors opened at the venue, a plethora of elderly people positively burst onto the pavements.

It was our memory café choir and we had been invited to sing at the cathedral. Our journey was exceptionally stressful. The coach driver had got lost and we were half an hour late.

The evening was good. There were formal choirs and barbershop outfits before us and they had the advantage over us – they knew what they were doing and they could sing. The criteria for our choir is simply that you have to be breathing.

As we came up on stage it took so long to get our people up there – complete with Zimmer frames – that the poor host did an impromptu interview with me.

But then we began to sing and something amazing happened. We were ancient but we had heart, and people began clapping. Then they broke out into song, joining in with us.

What had been a polite event, a professional event, became a heart event. I think that we touched people's hearts. Our obvious joy and vulnerability touched people. Plus, they knew the songs, and as we sang, they were given permission to let their hair down and join in with us. We know that singing has the power to uplift and soothe – just think of David singing to the mentally distressed Saul (1 Sam. 16:23). Our humble offering had the extraordinary sense of ushering us all into the presence of God.

What was obvious was the quality of the singing was secondary to the spirit of the singing. Plus, with our group of people with dementia and their carers, we had a message of hope.

Dementia doesn't define us. We are all bigger than that awful disease.

People couldn't quite believe our verve – the fact that we smiled and that our choir had people from different ethnicities. We were something that was good and that had such a powerful impact that I would call it magic, in the sense of a startling, sparkling delight.

Our little band of wounded soldiers inspired people with an odd wonder, and that wonder unlocked a deep joy that moved us all.

At the end of our set, the whole audience rose as one and gave us a standing ovation.

One of the people in the audience said to me that it was the best fun they had experienced for years. This was good because it was also the best fun we had had as well. I was approached by the children and grandchildren of one of our singers. They were so proud of their family member.

Wonder isn't just about a feeling. It affirms something – that we matter, that there is something joyous at the heart of things and that even a beautiful bunch of old people still have the fire to be happy.

Thinking about it, our turn at the cathedral was almost a picture-perfect example of wonder.

As we shuffled up to the stage, I am sure there was some trepidation in the audience. What would you expect from us? Possibly something not very good. What no one expected was an explosion of joy, jollity and love. The old songs stirred the hearts, and even the many youngsters who weren't familiar with them joined in the best they could. It was certainly unfamiliar – I'm not sure the last time the cathedral heard these old classics.

The Christian narrative often talks about light overcoming darkness. That darkness is more metaphorical than physical – indeed, it can be a problematic image for those with a visual impairment. I read it as being about the great battle between darkness and light.

To me, at least, that great cosmic battle between the opposing forces of good and evil rings absolutely true. And here we are, in some ways, part of that same struggle – both within us and also in our relationships, communities and world.

Our choir lifting hearts against substantial odds was a small victory in the battle of light against dark. There are little skirmishes going on all the time. It was a statement that dementia is not the end of all hope.

Our choir lifting hearts against substantial odds was a small victory in the battle of light against dark.

All the staff at the cathedral turned out at the end to escort us to our coach. It was quite a sight amid the busy bars and nightlife of Borough Market. Fully robed vergers and other helpers shepherded us back through a part of the greatest city in the world to our coach. Revellers stopped to look and ask us what we had been doing. (It is exceptionally poignant that in these same places, just a while later, extremists launched a murderous attack on innocent bystanders.)

As we pulled away, they waved us goodbye. We crossed the bridge over the River Thames. To our right, the impossibly beautiful city was a place of light and wonder. There was Tower Bridge and the various skyscrapers. On the coach, these faithful elders, most of whom had lived through the Blitz and all the social changes that have come, and taken it all in their stride, made themselves comfortable.

Suddenly a voice was raised as we were looking at the great city around us. 'Let's have a sing-song.'

And so, as our charabanc made its way home, we had one last blast of 'Maybe It's Because I'm a Londoner'. How fitting. London: that great symbol of hope that the Nazis couldn't kill, nor the extremists; where our songs were more powerful than any ideology of hate. That is a wonder indeed. I didn't want the night to end – I carry the wonder with me still.

Study Questions

Our choir lifting hearts against substantial odds was a small victory in the battle of light against dark. There are little skirmishes going on all the time. It was a statement that dementia is not the end of all hope.

Discuss. Where have you encountered hope in seemingly impossible situations?

And so, as our charabanc made its way home, we had one last blast of 'Maybe It's Because I'm a Londoner'. How fitting. London: that great symbol of hope that the Nazis couldn't kill, nor the extremists; where our songs were more powerful than any ideology of hate. That is a wonder indeed. I didn't want the night to end – I carry the wonder with me still.

What wonder do you carry with you, and why? What examples from your own life do you have of simply wonderful, magical experiences?

Prayer

*Fill us with hope, Lord, when the world seems
dangerous. Help us to see the potential and talents
of older people and to celebrate their lives.
We welcome outbreaks of joy and jollity and ask
that we might be the cause of these. Help us to
sing. To sing the song of heaven and of earth and of
all the wondrous things around us.
Thank you for our cities and our cathedrals and
all who work to make them places where we can
feel welcome.*

7

The Wonder of the Saints

Why should we spend a while pursuing the saints? Well, because they are examples of faith applied, and in their oddness, they help us to see again the possibilities of the life lived more fully and in colour.

Saints all present us with the challenge of those words of St Paul: 'Be imitators of me, as I am of Christ' (1 Cor. 11:1, NRSVA). That's what they have most in common.

Looking back, one thing I realize is that most of my time in church has been totally stripped of saints. By which I mean, established, acknowledged saints.

Of course, it has so many other things – great worship experiences, excellent preaching and huge amounts of love and friendship.

I guess my experience would be pretty typical of going to an evangelical church. I am not sure I quite understand our squeamishness about the saints, but perhaps it comes from a fear that they might distract us from the real deal, Jesus.

But actually, we *did* have our saints, and we read accounts of their lives although we just didn't call them saints. There was Brother Yun and the stirring account of his life, *The Heavenly Man*.[1] Yun went from half-starved boy from a poor village to mighty evangelist, despite massive opposition. He was one of our church's heroes.

Then we had Jackie Pullinger and her book *Chasing the Dragon*.[2] Her autobiography details her inspiring mission in the drug dens amid the poverty and violence of Hong Kong. Who wouldn't be inspired to think more deeply about what it is to be a Christian with such a stellar example? We could add to the list people like Billy Graham and his beautiful musing on final years, *Nearing Home*.[3]

It was standard practice as part of our journey as followers of Christ to take inspiration from those who were doing the Christian life well. But we never called them saints. I think we were worried about being too prideful about regular humans. And, of course, on occasion we reminded ourselves of the everyday saints that we ourselves were[4] – although with due caution.

The secular world, it seems, is also looking for saints. We all need our heroes and narratives of triumph over adversity. Michelle Obama's engaging autobiography *Becoming*[5] has sold a huge number of copies. It is a sobering thought that the ex-president's partner is more likely to sell out a stadium venue (pre-Covid!) in the UK than any visiting Christian evangelist.

Feet of clay

One of the reasons that saints fell into disrepute were accounts of their lives that painted them as paragons of virtue. With our modern knowledge of the brokenness of the church and its heroes, we simply felt that such virtue was not believable.

St Peter is the perfect saint. He has courage failures (Matt. 14:22–33), he says the wrong things (Matt. 16:22,23), he disowns his friend and leader (Matt. 26:73–5). He is a saint and not superman.

If we expect our saints to be paragons of virtue, then we misunderstand their very nature. St Paul encourages people to imitate him (1 Cor. 4:16). In his actions, he is hoping that they might be strengthened and learn something of Christ. Paul, perhaps like no other character in the Bible, knew all about his failings. Paul saw himself as 'the worst' of all sinners (1 Tim. 1:15). The worst person who ever lived.

However, he knew that by God's grace he was a saint – battered, beaten and bruised, but a saint with feet of clay. Perhaps that's why we can identify so well with him. He is so real that we begin to see how *we* might live a holy life despite being far from holy and full of flaws. It is through him that we ponder how we might be people of wonder even when everything seems to be going wrong. Saints – and that includes everyday saints like you and me – are saints not so much for what they have done, but because of what God did, and what he continues to do in and through them. By some odd miracle, God decides to use very ordinary, broken and sinful people to be his ambassadors.

I was in Scotland to do some writing. I was staying in a small flat which had a concierge. One day I had a great hour or so talking to him. He was very interested in faith and God and had many questions. It was one of those conversations where we feel we might have made a difference to another person's life. I felt rather pleased with myself, I suppose.

Later that day I stopped my writing and decided to prepare a snack. Of all things, I had bought a pack of bagels which were apparently packed with ingredients that were used in the far-distant past. I suppose the idea was to help us to be as healthy as our cave-dwelling ancestors. They plugged into our yearning for artisan products and food authenticity.

But fate intervened. In an unfamiliar kitchen, a bluntish knife slipped while I was cutting the bagel and I sliced off part of the top of my finger. Feeling suddenly lightheaded, I called the concierge, who came to my room with a first-aid kit.

To be fair, he had no first-aid training and I had no idea what he should do. He then grabbed my hand and ran the deep cut directly under the boiling water from the tap. My earlier holiness was gone in a moment and I let out an Anglo-Saxon exclamation. Our forebears would indeed have been proud of it.

When I got back from hospital a bit later, I felt bad about myself and reflected on what a flimsy saint I was. I decided to go down and apologize to my friend at the front desk. I was stunned when he smiled and told me that he hadn't realized that vicars were just like everyone else, and he couldn't wait to tell his friends. He said that if all vicars were like me, he might even think about going to church!

Perhaps it really was a moment of wonder – both from him (who was confounded by the beauty of my swearing) and me, who suddenly realized that I didn't need to be perfect. I was in good company in relation to saints and their feet of clay.

Dealing with objections

There are objections to the saints, and we must take them seriously. N.T. Wright, in his book *The Resurrection of the Son of God*,[6] worries that picking out any particular saintly individuals and celebrating their lives detracts from the significance of Christ. He is not alone in this view.

There are other objections. When we look at the saints themselves, many seem to be very poor examples indeed, and many seem not to have existed at all and were simply made up. Fictional saints wouldn't seem to be much good.

But there are good reasons to rehabilitate the saints. The saints allow us to see the faith in context. The Bible is culturally and historically conditioned. The saints can help us to see some of the ways people worked out the struggles of being a Christian in a range of different situations and at different times of history. Reading our Bible, we don't see, for instance, how the vocation of women can be easily followed – but in the life of the saints we can trace some of the contours.

Everyday saints

Jesus himself would have learned from the everyday saints around him as he grew up. His local rabbi, his parents and friends would have helped him to see the faith in action and would have inspired him. In that he was very like us.

There is a false distinction between official and unofficial saints. The official saints are often well known, and we gain from them because we often may have accounts of their lives. We feel they are the A-listers. And their stories are indeed stirring and surprising. Many people have a particular favourite who means a lot to them. But in God's eyes even a famous saint like St Francis is of no greater worth and stature than any of God's less well-documented children.

We are promised in the book of Revelation[7] that one day we will take part in a heavenly banquet with all the saints. My feeling is that we are as likely to be sat next to someone we have never heard of as one of the celebrities!

Some of the great unsung saints you might find yourself sat next to are Peter and Joan. They lugged an enormous drum kit that they kept in their garage every week to a service that their embryonic church was running. It was horrible work. The kit was heavy and the trip to the car required getting it down three flights of stairs. They got to the service first every week and left last. It was a huge commitment because the couple were in their early seventies and retired. The spare bedroom was now inhabited by the kit so no one could stay. But the kit was vital because the music in the new church was one of the main ways that it attracted the students from the medical school next door.

Over the months the church grew, despite some tricky moments along the way. Inside three years, the church moved to a lecture theatre in the medical school and began to attract 200 people. Drummers played the kit without realizing the commitment it took to get the great big thing there.

Without their amazing sacrifice, the church might have struggled. They did their service without pay or complaint and were a kind of father and mother to the church and the young pastors.

I would like to be sat next to them at the heavenly banquet. At last they might be able to give vent to what a pain the kit was and how they felt weary with the lifting. They might talk about the way it finished off one of their cars. But probably they'd be much more interested in encouraging me and listening to my story, because that was what they were like.

Saint-spotting

Robert Llewelyn, in his book *The Joy of the Saints*,[8] argues that saints from whatever tradition, well known, or obscure, or everyday, in fact all sing from the same hymn sheet. It is a helpful insight because we need to see what makes a saint.

His list of common traits includes that the saints' lives are mirrors, windows into the depths of God's compassion and show that God is not there to blame humankind. They live out and give voice to the constancy of God's love and the importance of forgiving one another. They don't duck the issue of the appalling effect of sin on ourselves, loved ones and the world, or the reality of God's justice. And all are marked by a life of prayer. They give us some hope that we, too, can be holy in our own odd and contradictory lives.

There is a quote attributed to Irenaeus – 'the glory of God is a person fully alive' – and although that is actually a mis-quote from the original Latin, it is the saints who most live out

> The person fully alive is the same person who leaves a trail of light.

this stirring vision. The person fully alive is the same person who leaves a trail of light.

I have known people like this and I am happy to claim a kind of informal sainthood for them. When I first became a Christian, I was so impressed with the sheer life and joy I experienced from people in the charis-matic church I attended. I am inspired by them still. If you have gone through a long period of being down, then seeing the opportunity for a life that might burst back into growth is most appealing. It amazed me to see people who were so happy to be at church. My memory of church came from my time as a boy, dragged along to our local one with my family.

The church was always cold, the hymns dreary and the sermon well beyond me. Most of all, I remember how miserable and uptight people seemed. Dare I say, they also seemed quite posh and not too interested in my working-class family. My mother told me that we all stopped going to church because my father felt that people were turning their noses up at us.

The church I went to as a teenager felt miserable and the people there looked miserable, or at least I thought so. When I went to the Pentecostal church in my forties, I was simply amazed at how happy people seemed to be in church. People smiled, as if we were long-lost friends coming home. There was joy in the house and boy, did my wounded little family need that. I found myself looking forward to going to church on a Sunday and wouldn't miss a week. It was the people as much as the music and preaching. But we were still struggling back at home.

One night I was at home looking after my wife, who was ill. There was a knock on the door and it was my pastors. I was filled with joy. Why on earth would they put themselves out for us? I know that our pastors would hate to be called Saints with a big S, but that is how they felt to us in our hours of need. They seemed like lifesavers and we were both amazed and grateful. It was a beautiful act. The only other people who had been there to help us before were our families.

Widening the circle of saints

A thought niggles me. In the many days before I was a Christian, what would I have made of all this? I am sure I would want to broaden the circle of saints – to claim those who had been bearers of light and hope in my life as the saints they were.

I would want to claim the truly unconventional and slightly crazy people who have been part of my life. The grumpy ones. The ones who sailed close to the wind and had an 'interesting' attitude to liberating the property of others. I would want to claim a bunch of heavy drinkers and pious abstainers. There would be teachers aplenty, and friends and relatives and the odd woman who rescued me when I had a funny turn in the local park as a boy. My hamster (yes) had just been put down and I felt all faint.

If saints do truly come in all shapes, sizes and dispositions, then I could assemble a motley army of sinners who were saints, and saints who were sinners.

I remember my friend Adrian who taught me what it was to love music and left me in awe at his musical genius. I remember him, his bottle of wine on the dashboard of my car, opening the window and engaging in odd conversations with passers-by. Adrian, who threw himself under a train. My hero with feet of clay. Who left that desperate message, found only when he died, about how much he had battled with his own demons and thoughts.

I remember the teacher who had always seemed difficult, who came to my house during the school holidays to help me to be brave enough to go to university when I had decided that I couldn't leave Northolt.

They loom into view as I think of these everyday saints. Like ghosts. And I think of a mentor who, despite losing his beloved teenage son to leukaemia, rang me every day to make sure that I was OK. Why did I never ask how he was? Why did I not comfort him in his grief? I was scared of hearing the answer, perhaps. I was selfish. But those calls, every day for three years, helped me to stay as sane as I was going to get in those dark days.

Study Questions

[Saints] are examples of faith . . .

How do you respond to this? Are you suspicious of 'traditional' saints and feel they might distract us from the main act – Jesus?

If saints do truly come in all shapes, sizes and dispositions, then I could assemble a motley army of sinners who were saints, and saints who were sinners.

Which people have you come across who are saintly, and why? How have they had an impact on your life?

Prayer

Thank you for the saints! Thank you for the well-known ones and the unsung ones too. We feel wonder at the saints who have been on our life's journey with us – those who have encouraged us by their examples and helped us along our way.
Help us to be open to the very idea of saints and not fear that our acknowledgement of them might take us away from Jesus.
We name now the saints who have meant so much to us . . .
Thank you for the great body of saints who have gone before us and that we can read about their lives. Thank you, too, for the unlikely saints, the scruffy ones, the broken ones, the saints who struggled with their faith and yet kept on – one step after the other.
Thank you for the great secular saints of our age – doctors, nurses, teachers, social workers, barristers, physiotherapists, bus drivers, shop workers, delivery people, and all those who care for others.
Open us up to the saints of our church – the spirit of their life and what it might teach us.

8

The Wintry Grief of the Shoemaker

One of the teachers of the law came and heard them debating. Noticing that Jesus had given them a good answer, he asked him, 'Of all the commandments, which is the most important?' 'The most important one,' answered Jesus, 'is this: "Hear, O Israel: the Lord our God, the Lord is one. Love the Lord your God with all your heart and with all your soul and with all your mind and with all your strength." The second is this: "Love your neighbour as yourself." There is no commandment greater than these.'

Mark 12:28–31

There are three short words that are easy to say but difficult to live. *I love you.*

They are difficult because they involve risk. When we consent to be loved and to love others, then we will be hurt or our loved ones will be hurt and sometimes all we will be able to do is to be present in that hurt.

'I love you' means that we will not go away if loving someone else becomes tough. It means that we will put someone else's wellbeing ahead of our own. That kind of love is full of wonder because it does not make sense at all.

Humans seem to have a propensity to selfishness and jealousy. When we see virtue, we find it hard to cope with. It is always easier to join a mob and shout vitriol or call names.

Another way of putting it is that sin is the greatest cancer of all. In a world where we all suffer from this cancer, then sacrificial love doesn't make much sense.

There is a temptation to dress up the world. We insulate ourselves from what is around us. But we live in a world which can often be judging, cruel and unfair, full of resentment and hatred. Our addiction to social media has perhaps sharpened the cruelty that we can deliver to others. This can have a hor-rible cost.

Love that involves sacrifice shines into this world as a great last hope. It may not bring a miracle cure for Alzheimer's, or poverty, or bullying, but it is a great last stand. Just as the cross seemed like a last stand against all the forces of evil lined up against the Christ.

The rehabilitation of Martin

In his short story *Where Love Is, There God Is Also*, Tolstoy introduces us to Martin.[1] Martin is a shoe-maker. He is known for his professionalism and high standards and he is always busy. He stays in his base-ment where he does the work with just a single win-dow out onto the street. Indeed, so obsessed is he with shoes that he can recognize the passers-by just by their footwear.

His cramped conditions and claustrophobic life hint at a deeper malaise. Martin is in a deep and unen-durable grief. It is a grief that has pushed him in on himself. He is alone. His wife died years earlier and all his children too, except for a 3-year-old son. And then, after he dedicated himself to looking after his precious son, the boy died as well.

In deep snowed-in grief, Martin denied God and railed against him. Where is there to go from such a place?

One day he meets a man who is a missionary. They talk, and the missionary tells him of the sufferings he endures. He encourages Martin towards a change of heart, and the cobbler responds by buying a Bible and reading the Gospel of Luke.

Martin's lonely life begins to take on a little colour. He reads his Bible and begins to feel a bit happier. He has started to turn a corner towards his recovery (it is a recovery I have seen mirrored many times).

One night, Martin reads the passage about the Pharisee who invited Jesus to visit him in his house. He realizes that he has closed himself off from the love of God.

As Martin sleeps, he hears God's voice saying that he intends to visit him tomorrow. In the morning, scepticism has taken hold.

Martin has a series of encounters with people who are lost, desperate and in need of love and help. There is the old man, penniless and shovelling snow. Martin treats him to a warm drink. Indeed, Martin speaks movingly about God to the old man and heals him as much in soul as body.

Then comes an impoverished woman – freezing cold and with a child. She has the wrong clothes for the weather and is in despair. Martin gives her clothes and money and speaks to her as well about Jesus.

Finally, he finds himself in a different situation. He mediates between an old woman and a boy who steals her apples. He shows compassion to both and helps them to become reconciled and see what is wrong in their lives. The bitterness of the woman evaporates and the boy helps her on her way. It is a picture of reconciliation.

Back in his room Martin wonders why God didn't keep his promise and meet up with him. At that point the three figures he had helped appear in his home. They point out that when he helped them, he had been helping God himself.

The scales fall from his eyes and he realizes that he has indeed met with God. The story has many resonances. It explains the miracle of reconciliation and the pain of losing people we love. It shows the winter that can descend that pulls us away from human contact and the slow path back towards connection with God, ourselves and each other.

But at its very heart is the wondrous insight that where love is, God is. That may be one of the great lifesavers. When all has gone wrong in my life and I am feeling far from God and unable to pray, I head for the company of those I love or try to spend time offering love to others.

The wonder of sacrificial love

Each week I run a memory café at my church. It has become a place of love and hope and is a bit of a wonder. On the one hand, just seeing so many people having their lives changed is awesome and never fails to amaze. A simple cup of tea, companionship and singing can have an extraordinary impact. Who would have thought it?

But there's something else. Every week we see people in the throes of an illness that could only come from the depths of hell, surrounded by the love of people who refuse to give up on them.

Dementia is not the end of hope. Not because there is a cure, because there isn't yet. But because it cannot defeat the love of family and friends who refuse to give up on people who no longer recognize them and have slipped away bit-by-bit.

The great sadness is that the carers know what is happening and know where it will lead. But person after person has told me that they took their marriage vows and they meant them. And so each week, tenderly they bring their loved ones, lost to a far shore, and do all they can to make their lives a little better.

But is it tough? Yes, it can be desperate and lead to deep despair, but reaching out and doing love is godly and precious and, yes, full of wonder.

Jesus looks after his mother

In Old English the word 'wundor' signified astonishment. That's an interesting resonance because it helps us with that sense of a kind of breakthrough moment. Most days I wander around in a dream, so a bit of astonishment certainly wouldn't go amiss.

One aspect of wonder is the impulse to think of others and look after them. It is easy to be callous and narcissistic, but the sacrificial care of others is a great calling.

> Near the cross of Jesus stood his mother, his mother's sister, Mary the wife of Clopas, and Mary Magdalene. When Jesus saw his mother there, and the disciple whom he loved standing near by, he said to her, 'Woman, here is your son,'

and to the disciple, 'Here is your mother.' From that time on, this disciple took her into his home.

John 19:25–7

Jesus is facing his death and is in agony. He has a date with destiny which involves nothing less than saving the world and everything in it. You'd probably imagine he'd be single-minded about it.

But there is a detail he has to sort out before he can carry on with his mission. It is easy to miss. He has a domestic matter to attend to. If he leaves his mum unlooked-after, she will face shame and ruin. But interestingly, it seems he cannot entrust her totally to his blood family.

And so, he does something very unusual. He carries out a beautiful exchange. He doesn't dump his mother on his young friend John. No, he entrusts each to the other. He hands over his mother to John as a new mother to him. He hands over John to Mary as a new son.

He ensures that both will be comforted and both will gain from a new flowering and a new compassionate connection.

It is as though the heavenly battle that had to be raging stops for a moment. The dramatic mood music pauses. And the bloodied and battered Christ carries out an act of huge tenderness and love.

When I see people looking after their mothers and fathers at memory café, or going out of their way to help others, I am reminded of this everyday drama at the cross.

Christ's life was full of kindness and gentleness. He modelled a sacrificial love and we are encouraged to be imitators of him.

But when we see this kind of sacrificial love acted out in our communities and everyday activities, surely it causes us to pause and wonder. Why on earth do we do it? It would be far easier not to, and much less messy. But despite all we read in the newspapers and see online, sacrificial love is still the dominant force in the world.

Anyone can love another when there is nothing to lose from it. We can all showboat and virtue-signal. But what about when the going gets hard and every step is difficult?

What Jesus said

Jesus said, 'Whoever finds their life will lose it, and whoever loses their life for my sake will find it' (Matt. 10:39).

It is an odd statement, perhaps, one that has para-dox at its heart and for linear thinkers, as we tend to be, it is tough to unravel. And yet wonder tends to work and find its way into our lives when we break free of a straight line.

The statement swims against the tide of modern psychological thought. We tend to speak about fulfilling our selves, about self-actualization. The problem with this is that it makes us ill. We strive for the perfect life and the perfect everything and can only feel the hollowness at the core of this doctrine. Our egos can be a big barrier to being better, because there will always be something out there to torpedo our 'selves'.

Jesus proposes a different way, and it is one that many people have found leads to a new way of looking at the world and at what we are here to do. Rather than serve ourselves, why not serve others?

Eighteenth-century thinkers had an inkling of this. They proposed that altruism was the great cure. It made others feel good and us feel good as well. But what Jesus talks about is a step-up from altruism.

If we are prepared to be among the pain and suffering of others, carrying our own as lightly as we can, we can do the work we are called to do. Sacrificial service is a way of life and not an easy one. It may run counter to our culture, but when we see it, we see the truth of it, and we know that it is the only way to really escape the prison of our selves. Oddly, if we chase self-actualization, it has a habit of eluding us. Losing ourselves and putting others first is a road to a kind of wonder that can help to heal us.

> Losing ourselves and putting others first is a road to a kind of wonder that can help to heal us.

A friend of mine wrote a book about this that has stayed by my side for years. In *Finding Calcutta*[2] she explains how, in the midst of personal turmoil, she wrote to Mother Teresa of Calcutta. After an exchange of letters Mary, my friend, set off to 'serve' in Calcutta with Mother Teresa. But things did not go as she had planned. She was extremely squeamish of the suffering she found – and began by living at a nearby hotel. She could cope here because it was sanitized and just like home. She was able to keep the suffering of others, and her own psychological wounds, at arm's length.

She found it especially hard to be in the presence of young children and babies. She had gone through an abortion in an earlier period of her life, and she had compensated by sealing herself off from younger days. Mother Teresa made it so that Mary would actually confront this fear, and despite earlier revulsion, she developed a deep bond with a very severely disabled boy. They became inseparable, and her early revulsion at his condition gave way to something that was very beautiful.

But who was doing the ministering and to whom? It is a question I often ask myself as a parish priest. When I have an encounter with someone who seems broken and lost, it only serves to remind me of my own lostness, and each time I feel that I gain more in terms of healing than the person I am called to listen to.

But there was more to come. Because Mary realized that she had her own Calcutta to minister into – it was one back on her doorstep. Going to India just displaced the real need for sacrificial service in her home country.

Mary is a professor in a deeply secular university in the United States. She found *her* Calcutta right there and now ministers to the broken and fragile students, who are wealthy beyond measure but truly poor spiritually.

Her book is very challenging. It asks us to consider where we might find our own Calcutta. Where are the areas of need in our communities where we are called to set aside ego and simply be the person who is there with those who need us? Are there places that we are scared to go to because they remind us of past failures and hurts?

Sacrificial lives

It's the Christmas of 1945 in Bedford Falls, New York, and George Bailey is facing an existential crisis of epic proportions. He has given over his whole life to others and yet he now faces financial ruin and has decided to take his own life. Was it all worth it? What difference did he make, and might the world have been a better place without him?

You may recognize the scenario from Frank Capra's Christmas favourite, *It's a Wonderful Life*, released in 1946. The film stars the incomparable James Stewart as George Bailey and, despite not being an overnight success, has come to be known as one of the truly great films. That is surely because it is a film that truly understands wonder in so many of its dimensions.

George has given up on his own interests on numerous occasions to help others. As a boy he rescued his brother from drowning and so loses the hearing in one ear. His dreams of college and a round-the-world trip disappear when he agrees to take over the family loan company on the death of his father. Even his honeymoon goes up in smoke when he uses the money to pay for it to save a run on the bank.

But despite it all, things seem to have come to a head when his forgetful uncle mislays the loan company's money, due to the machinations of slum landlord and crook, Henry Potter.

Thankfully, there is a trainee angel on hand to help George. Clarence Odbody earns his wings by showing George something very profound indeed. George gets to see something that the rest of us may never see – what the world would have been like if he had never existed. It is sobering. George realizes that without his humble efforts, Bedford Falls would have been a story of misery and a place where the bad guys won.

In a way, George lived out Jesus' great teaching. He gained his life through putting others first (through losing it). But there is more here.

The film shows the ultimate significance of each and every one of us. Many of us do not know the names of our great-grandparents, but without them we would not be here at all. Every single one of us makes a difference and so we form part of an awe-inspiring chain of causality. Our actions here and now matter, even if we can't see the results they had or will have.

George is an interesting character in the context of the time in which the film was made and released. The film is set right at the end of the war. Indeed, one of the dynamics is that George sees himself as a bit of a failure. He was unable to take up military service because of his deafness. But his brother Harry is a navy pilot war hero – having received the Medal of Honor for shooting down a kamikaze pilot.

The town is waiting to welcome back Harry in a fanfare of glory. But George has missed out on all this.

The subtle message for an America about to move on from the war is that our new heroes might be people like George, as well as the established ones like Harry. The heroes of the reconstruction of a world ruined by war are going to be those who are prepared to sacrifice their own interests to help others – those who live in slum housing, are bereaved or face penury.

In his time, the Jewish people were disappointed in Jesus. They wanted a mighty warrior like David. Many wanted a fighter who would rid the country of oppressive masters – who can blame them?

Sacrificial love has always been countercultural. We expect bombs and might to bring about change.

George's brush with wondering whether to commit suicide and his subsequent rehabilitation help him to realize something very important about his own significance.

If a sequel were made, it would be wonderful to know what the rest of his life held in store for him. How might Bedford Falls have been further transformed?

Study Questions

Each week I run a memory café at my church. It has become a place of love and hope and is a bit of a wonder. On the one hand, just seeing so many people having their lives changed is awesome and never fails to amaze. A simple cup of tea, companionship and singing can have an extraordinary impact. Who would have thought it?

What examples of sacrificial love have you experienced? How have they changed your life?

'When Jesus saw his mother there, and the disciple whom he loved standing near by, he said to her, "Woman, here is your son," and to the disciple, "Here is your mother." From that time on, this disciple took her into his home.'

Discuss. How does this help us understand the way we can help and care for others? Have you had times in your life when you have been mentored or cared for by other people?

Jesus said, 'Whoever finds his life will lose it, and whoever loses his life for my sake will find it.'

What do you make of Jesus' words?

Prayer

Love is victorious, dear Lord. You showed us that by your cross and resurrection. We acknowledge, though, that love is about sacrifice and risk. The risk of being hurt, the risk of being separated from the ones we love by death.

Can you help us to appreciate the sacrificial love of others – our parents, guardians, carers, family and friends? Let us celebrate all those who have put themselves out for us and have been there when we most needed them.

Help us to offer sacrificial love to others – to put our love for you and our neighbours at the front of what we do. Let us see examples of love around us and be inspired by it, talk about it and celebrate it as a mirror of the divine love for all people.

Help us to say sorry to those we have hurt and to have time to make amends; to be able to help them and show love towards them.

9

The Little Church Around the Corner

Where might you find a little burst of wonder amid the scale and bustle of mid-town Manhattan? The obvious answer is in the extraordinary landscape here – the canyons and the cliffs of steel and glass. It truly is one of those places that is exactly what you want it to be.

But on a rainy day, with the world rushing by, it is easy to be beaten back by the noise and clamour. If you are ever passing this way, I recommend that you do as I did and spend a while at an extraordinary little church that offers a radical alternative to the world as it is.

Early days

It was on the first Sunday in October 1848 that the first service at the Church of the Transfiguration was held. It was held in a private home at 48 East 24th Street in Manhattan. The following year the church was built on what was then the outskirts of the city.

These days, the city has swallowed up the fields and brooks and the church stands with the Empire State Building virtually in its back yard. Over the years the church sheltered escaped slaves during the draft riots of the Civil War and provided food for hungry people. It has always had a connection with actors, being just a short walk to Broadway.

It also became known as 'the little church around the corner' when the then rector agreed to perform the wedding of an actor and his partner in 1870. Only the 'little church around the corner' would do it, and the name stuck. (Actors were seen as flighty and not very respectable.)

These days

You'll see the beautiful garden first and then you'll notice a rather beautiful single-storey church. Most days there will be more people in the garden than the church. This green lung attracts workers on their lunch hour and people just wanting to stop and read or look at the plants.

It's the garden which is the first clue of the wonder in this place. It's mainly ground cover but there are little pockets and crannies of planting. Plus, there is a charming plaque to a beloved vicarage cat that graced the place and blessed the people.

Inside the church, of course, the wonder continues with an arts and crafts masterpiece. It's full of wood panelling, icons and brass and a depth of prayerful peace that is impossible to ignore.

The church is an oasis of beauty and the Anglo-Catholic tradition, which points to another source of wonderment. I am glad to report that God is alive and well and walking the corridors in this beautiful place.

I am greeted by the effervescent priest, Father John. He's suffering from a bad back but tells me that adrenalin has taken over and he's trying to ignore it. We talk about wonder in his beautiful vicarage right next to the church.

But Father John is no aesthete; he knows the harsh realities of life in NYC. He tells me that just a few days ago a drug addict broke into the church through a skylight and stole money and damaged the church. The beauty of this little wonder is very much part and parcel of the messiness of life in one of the busiest, most beautiful and brutal cities on the planet.

We talk about why Manhattan, with all its money and success stories, still needs the church, and especially this church which follows the ancient Book of Common Prayer and features vicars in black cassocks. It feels like a church, which is important in a city with its Trump Towers and other temples to acquisition.

'In God that which is ancient never becomes old,' Father John tells me. There is something in the ancient words and beautiful church full of icons and symbols that draws the modern mind.

'People are panting – almost screaming – for the filling of the God void. They come here and the ancient rituals touch them. They might just come in and look at the altar, or sit awhile. It is as though their souls are porous and they absorb something of God here.'

He shares with me that the wondrous power of the ancient words seems to have been found in a Collect (or special prayer) which goes like this:

> ALMIGHTY God, unto whom all hearts be open, all desires known, and from whom no secrets are

hid: Cleanse the thoughts of our hearts by the inspiration of thy Holy Spirit, that we may perfectly
love thee, and worthily magnify thy holy Name;
through Christ our Lord. Amen.

The Book of Common Prayer
Reproduced with permission of Cambridge
University Press through PLSclear[1]

John explains that he grew up in the South and was,
at first, a charismatic evangelical Christian. He keeps
still the great sense of a close and personal God
from those early days. But as he grew older, he was
attracted 'as a moth towards the flame' by something of the beauty of The Book of Common Prayer.

And here he is now holding together Catholic and
Protestant traditions in this beautiful, wondrous little church. How does he experience God here?

'I have come to see that you can experience God in
the routines of faith. He is in them. As I unlock the
door each day for one of the three services, I experience God. When I walk through the darkened church
or open the prayer book, God is there. It is as I go
through the daily routines that I walk alongside God
and it seems wonderful to me, even if I feel empty.'

Sometimes, perhaps often, Father John conducts his
daily services alone – with no customers. The busy
city is going about its business. But the church has

stood here for many years and it feels like the city needs it as much as it needs the city.

As I sit through an early morning service listening to Thomas Cranmer's words, I am suddenly alive with God's presence. I feel as though I can barely move. Afterwards I wonder what it all means.

We put so much effort into designing new services with so many different and 'exciting' elements. We pray freely and wait on the action of the Holy Spirit. And yet in these ancient words and in this quiet, dignified holy place, God seems to be alive and well and opening his arms to all.

As I leave, Father John shakes my hand and says, 'Go well, brother, and remember to be kind; your actions may be the only Bible the people you meet read today.'

This is a place of kindness in a place that can seem angular and cruel. Just around the corner a man is lying unconscious on the streets. He has no shoes. Seeing his bare feet, he seems so vulnerable; it hits me that once he was a child in his mother's arms. He was once a source of wonderment to someone somewhere. To the weeping

> To the weeping Christ, this lost man is still a source of wonder.

Christ, this lost man is still a source of wonder. God has the memory of all that he has been, is now and all that will be.

Lying on his front, the man has taken the trouble to pull out the linings of his trouser pockets to show he has nothing worth stealing.

Study Questions

This is a place of kindness in a place that can seem angular and cruel. Just around the corner a man is lying unconscious on the streets. He has no shoes. Seeing his bare feet, he seems so vulnerable; it hits me that once he was a child in his mother's arms. He was once a source of wonderment to someone somewhere. To the weeping Christ, this lost man is still a source of wonder. God has the memory of all that he has been, is now and all that will be.

Discuss.

Prayer

Thank you for all who minister in our cities and to vulnerable people. Help us to see our fellow citizens in all their wondrous beauty, however their life is at the moment. We pray for our priests and for all they do – for every priest who prays alone in their church.
Thank you that even in a place like New York, with all its business power, The Little Church Around the Corner is there spreading the love of God.

10

A Burning Bush and a Holy Place

Moses was no regular shepherd. In fact, he had begun his life in very different circumstances – adopted into the Egyptian royal family and blessed by privilege. But to say that things have gone wrong would be an understatement.

These days he is being exploited by his father-in-law and leading a life of monotony. Each day is similar to the last and things don't look like changing any time soon. The very last thing Moses is expecting is a meeting with God. Thankfully he is not in a day-dream and is paying attention.

He spots an odd sight. There is a bush which is on fire, but the bush seems untouched by the flames. It would be easy to pass on by, to not be curious or to attribute it to some mundane cause. So often we live in a dream or refuse to open ourselves up to the unusual.

When God sees that Moses has decided to take a look at the strange phenomenon, he calls him from within the bush. And so begins an encounter which will change this man's life.

God realizes that Moses is taking note. Rather than launch into a speech, God does something very simple and beautiful.

> When the LORD saw that he had gone over to look, God called to him from within the bush, 'Moses! Moses!' And Moses said, 'Here I am.'
>
> Exodus 3:4

The Lord who made the universe uses Moses' name. He establishes a simple connection using the word that is most personal to Moses. In the connection Moses has stumbled onto holy ground – a thin place where God is close and our perceptions are changed. But also, in acknowledging Moses' personhood, God makes holy the nuts and bolts and actuality of Moses' life and humanity. If we can stand on holy ground, then we truly have something of the author of all goodness about us.

God tells Moses to take his shoes off and then introduces himself as though he were an everyday stranger exchanging pleasantries.

> 'Do not come any closer,' God said. 'Take off your sandals, for the place where you are standing is holy ground.' Then he said, 'I am the God of your father, the God of Abraham, the God of Isaac and the God of Jacob.'
>
> Exodus 3:5,6

God has a mission for Moses – to go to the dreaded Pharaoh and bring God's oppressed people to freedom. After some toing-and-froing Moses agrees to go, now assured that God is with him and will never desert him. The rest, as they say, is history.

What is perhaps most shocking about this life-changing encounter is the sheer ordinariness of it all. It takes place in the wilderness, on a regular day in a simple old bush. God is rational and everyday and speaks with Moses. The wonder isn't so much in the glory of God, but in the accessibility of the situation. Moses could surely echo Jacob when he said 'Surely the LORD is in this place, and I was not aware of it' (Gen. 28:16).

When Moses realizes that God is there, the ground under his feet becomes holy. It is as electrifying a moment as when the dejected followers break bread with Jesus in an equally ordinary setting (Luke 24:13–35). Perhaps the key is to be more open and to expect these encounters and recognize them when they are happening.

Everyday holy places

Moses' odd experience doesn't seem to be a one-off. I have spoken to dozens of people who have reported similar everyday encounters with God. I have come to think that they are much more common than people think. Although God-encounters may take place in everyday places, they themselves are often life-changing and feel miraculous.

While studying for ordination I used to ask all the visiting speakers the same question: 'When was the time you most experienced the presence of God?' It became something of a source of mirth among my fellow students – or perhaps annoyance. But I was asking because I was genuinely interested.

For most of my life I had considered myself an atheist. But I secretly longed for a moment that somehow transported me from the everyday. I think I knew that there was wonder out there, but it was like a long-lost friend who you can't quite remember any more.

When I had my own encounter with God, in a lecture theatre at Charing Cross Hospital, it was a shock, but it was the thing I had desired for my whole life. But each time I had felt that I might encounter God, I somehow drew back from the experience in an act of self-sabotage. But then I had my date with destiny in my forties.

What struck me about my conversion experience was how peaceful it felt. For weeks afterwards I felt as though I had new glasses – I was simply seeing the world differently. It was a place of wonder. Nothing seemed normal any more.

Somewhat typically, I began to be assailed by negative thoughts. I wondered if I might have made it all up – perhaps it was wish-fulfilment. Or perhaps I might let my mind winkle away and undermine what had happened. I was genuinely terrified that whatever had happened might wear off.

I went to see a friend who told me that my conversion experience was very genuine. I was so relieved and began to trust what had happened. My meeting with God in the lecture theatre had been the real deal. That's why I started asking seasoned priests about their holy moments. Each one reinforced my own experience.

One time, someone told me that they were just having an ordinary morning, having breakfast, when they suddenly felt the enormity of the presence of God. They felt as if their home was filled with God's loving presence. It seemed incredible to them that God had been there, sharing the meal. This odd encounter profoundly changed this person's life and outlook. This simple holy moment had not just boosted the faith of somebody who had been serving God faithfully for many years, but made them realize that God is even more mysterious and wonderful than they ever thought.

Another person told me that once, they opened the curtain in their living room, and as the sun shone in, they had a sense of God right with them, right there. Everything in the room, the dust, the light, everything was infused with holiness.

These everyday encounters and establishment of informal holy ground have an echo in Jesus' ministry (John 4:4–26). Jesus is thirsty and exhausted. He meets a Samaritan woman at one of her holy sites – Jacob's Well. Indeed, this had been a matter of contention between the Samaritans and the Jews.

For the Samaritans the mountain where the well was positioned was a holy site. The Jewish people claimed Jerusalem as theirs. It had, metaphorically, further poisoned relations between the two groups, who already had a history of conflict, and was one of those long-running religious disagreements that just get more and more entrenched.

Jesus says something very surprising. He says that the 'time is coming' when neither Jerusalem nor the well will be the place of ultimate holiness. When the Messiah comes, all that will be required will be to worship 'in the Spirit and in truth'.

Established holy places

Some places do seem to have a memory of all the prayer they have soaked up. Others just help us to feel closer to God and his creation.

Long before I was a Christian I used to go with my wife to the West Country. Each time we would visit a very beautiful wood with some ancient trees. We would wait till no one was around and then give the trees a hug. It was very beautiful – the meeting between us and what we felt were these wise and comforting old trees.

You might cry 'pantheism' or 'New Age', or whatever. But I don't think it was either of these. The dear old trees felt more than simply wood. We took comfort from our encounters with trees and we felt wonderment. At the time we were struggling with many issues and were feeling worn down – but these moments in the West Country were a kind of spiritual lung.

We had a sense that other people had enjoyed this place and that it had been special to them. I now think that this exposure to our tree friends was a way of softening us up for a bigger revelation – that they and the holy ground they occupied were and are even more marvellous than we thought.

We hear about a very animated creation – one that wants to sing God's praises. So perhaps these old trees were gently singing the praises of their creator and we had an intimation of this glorious truth?

When I first encountered God, I think that it felt comforting and beautiful because I had felt something of the same in my days as a tree-hugger. The feeling of wonder is a universal currency – it is one of the

> The feeling of wonder is a universal currency – it is one of the whispers of our immortality.

whispers of our immortality and the promise that one day the whole world will be made new.

People, it seems to me, have much more sense of the divine nature out and about in the natural world than they sometimes get in church. It is hard not to have some level of wonder at the mind-boggling beauty and complexity of our home planet. When the astronauts came home, they must have felt both ecstatic and bereft. They were part of the few who had seen the wonder of our home, but when back on dry land their wings were clipped and they were never to return to that great darkness in their rockets and landing modules.

The wonder of liminal spaces

There are places where the divide between heaven and earth, God and us, seems much thinner than normal. In these places we might be able to get a glimpse beyond our everyday troubles and preoccupations.

To get out of our spiritual and everyday rut, perhaps we can move into a sacred space or place. These are liminal places where we might ditch some of our certainties and face the risk of waiting and wondering.

Sometimes such a liminal space might be a traditional place of prayer and pilgrimage. But if we accept that the whole world is holy, then it could just as well be on the social housing estate we grew up in, or the office, or the kitchen. There is a beautiful democracy in holy places.

When Christ returns from the dead, he meets people as they go about their everyday life. He gate-crashes his friends when they are fishing. The last thing they expected was to meet him there. But when they do meet him, he is ready to share food with them, almost in a recreation of the Last Supper – and he creates a place of holiness right there on the shore (John 21).

In fact, he cooks them breakfast. Moses had to take his shoes off while he was on holy ground. His dirty feet would pollute it. But Christ changes the rules and the geography of holiness. As his dejected followers regroup, he frequently eats with them. He shows them the divine hospitality and he shows them, too, to expect holy places in the most ordinary of places. They come as they are and are not expected to take their shoes off.

On the shore by the lake where his friends made their living, Christ helps them to regain hope. He appears to them not as the mighty God with legions of angels, but as their friend who wants them to be fed and warm.

They want to feel safe again – even though many dangers will come their way. The best way they can do this is to sit on holy ground and be with the God who reassures them that what is past is past and that they have the strength to lead a generation of saints that will take his message and person into the future.

Sometimes we find ourselves in a 'thin' place – a place where God seems close and we can stop a while. These places can take us by surprise or, of course, we can deliberately go on pilgrimage towards them.

C.S. Lewis created a liminal space in his Narnia books. Perhaps he was looking for a way of showing that heaven is close, that God is in the room with us. Lewis was able to give us that sense of the imminent God and to open up the possibility that he is very close indeed. Above all, he wants to demolish the idea that God is somehow 'up there'. If there is no up there, how do we envisage God and where he is? If he is everywhere and in everything, then we open ourselves up to the kind of encounter that goes way beyond a God in the clouds waiting for the end times.

In the Narnia series the heroes enter into an old wardrobe.[1] It is a kind of gateway – a doorway. It is just a short step from there to another world. All that is needed is to be aware of the possibility and open to the adventure that is about to unfold.

What makes it so encouraging is that it is ordinary and everyday. Who would have imagined that a simple wardrobe was so special? It is a place of risk – the possibility is always there to turn back; but what is ahead, although far less certain, is the possibility of a new reality and change.

But is it all a place of worship?

Often, as I write this book, a cautionary voice makes itself heard. Isn't all this a kind of idolatry of place? Didn't Jesus come to free us all from anchoring of temples and holy places – all holiness is him, and the church is a set of people, not a building? Holiness is in people and not places. It is a serious concern and not one I want to dismiss.

Perhaps the answer lies in our understanding of the incarnation. Because Jesus was one of us, the material world is touched by holiness. The Christian faith is a material one – it doesn't separate the holy from the everyday. And when the holy family were clustered in a barn with the infant Christ, would we not have felt something of the closeness of God in that place?

Perhaps we can at least remain open to the idea that sometimes in some places we feel an amazing sense of wonder and that we can sometimes get a feeling of God there – be they a mighty cathedral, pilgrimage destination or the local tip?[2]

Timothy Radcliffe helped me to get a little closer to unravelling this conundrum:

> There was undoubtedly a trend in the earliest years to see Christ as having liberated us from holy places. Think of Jesus' speech to the Samaritan woman at the well, or Stephen's speech against the temple in Acts. But human beings are topophilic, needing homes on earth to imagine our final home. Good old St Thomas Aquinas reminded us that grace perfects nature and human nature needs places, shrines, pilgrimages, to root our sense of belonging. Pope Benedict in his *'[The] Spirit of the Liturgy*[3] did, though, point out that Christian liturgy, unlike that of Judaism and Islam, locates us not in space . . . but only in time . . . as we wait for the final coming of Christ.[4]

Study Questions

Moses' odd experience doesn't seem to be a one-off. I have spoken to dozens of people who have reported similar everyday encounters with God. I have come to think that they are much more common than people think. Although God-encounters may take place in everyday places, they themselves are often life-changing and feel miraculous.

Have you had an everyday encounter with God? What happened and what was it like? How did it make your feel?

When I had my own encounter with God, in a lecture theatre at Charing Cross Hospital, it was a shock, but it was the thing I had desired for my whole life.

Do you desire an encounter with God? Discuss. Have you been searching for this kind of experience?

To get out of our spiritual and everyday rut, perhaps we can move into a sacred space or place. These are liminal places where we might ditch some of our certainties and face the risk of waiting and wondering.

Can you think of any liminal spaces that you have encountered? What makes them so special?

Prayer

We live in an amazing world and within it are places that help us feel close to the source of all wonder – you. Open us up to finding the 'thin' places and seeing them everywhere we look.
Help us to find places of encounter and change on our doorsteps – on our estates and in the normal places that we go to. Thank you, too, for extraordinary places – holy places like Lindisfarne. Thank you for the centuries of prayer and service there.
Please honour all of us pilgrims. We are all journeying and wondering about our lives. We want to experience that unique sense of wonder much more often. Help all those who are seeking a moment of breakthrough, a time when they can start again.

11

God Among Us

I wrote this book because I had a sense that wonder is for all and is more than an experience. It is a way of looking at the world – open to all, but sharpened and made more beautiful and sustainable by a faith in Christ. And so I have looked mainly for the kind of common experiences that might point to wonder. These are places and experiences that show the democracy of wonder – although we so often lose sight of it.

> Wonder is for all and is more than an experience. It is a way of looking at the world.

If we accept that God was a person – not God pretending to be one, but just like us, although free from the sin that blights our lives – then we begin to see the people we share our lives with in a new way; a wondrous way.

It is as though we should see our fellow humans with a fresh sense of worth. By living out the incarnation, God conferred holiness on everyday life. Everyday life and people were not, are not, below God, because he lived out his life in a backwater with his family, working in their business and being a part of the world around him.

I find the incarnation so thrilling, and each time I come across an awkward or difficult person I try to remind myself of their innate holiness – chosenness. I then remind myself of how awkward and difficult I can be to others as well. I am certainly guilty of sometimes judging others, but I have no right to.

If the incarnation is about anything, it is about the wonder of the everyday, and of everyday people.

It is more than possible to be amazed by our fellow human beings without a sense of God. We can marvel at the mechanics of the human body. We can enjoy loving our family and friends. But, and this was true for me *before* I became a person of faith, we tend to judge others by certain standards – success, wealth, beauty, school and job.

Compassion is not the preserve of those with faith, nor is service to others. But what I know is that my sense of wonder has been sharpened by the God who was, and remains, a person. If that is true, then we can't look at people the same. Or at least, I can't.

Was God a mess?

When we read our Bibles we get a picture of Jesus; not as a proxy, but as a real person. And the more we read, the more extraordinary that picture becomes – and all the more comforting.

Jesus didn't carry a diary. We might call his ministry style 'unpredictable' if we are being kind. But I like to describe it as 'a mess' – thank God.

Just to pick a few examples – he turns up late for his friend Lazarus and the poor fellow dies. His friends even confront Jesus and ask why he couldn't have hurried himself up (John 11:21,32).

Jesus seems to me to be easily distracted; he speaks to unspeakable people. He is accused of being a drunkard and a glutton (Luke 7:34).

Jesus manages to wipe out the pig population in Gadara while showing mercy to demons who have taken up residence in a local man. Rather than wipe them out, he lets his demonic enemies inhabit 2,000 pigs, all of which are drowned (Mark 5:1–20). If you wanted to make an impact, wiping out the livestock industry wasn't a good idea.

So, I would like to claim the incarnated life as not being the perfectly organized one. I think that Jesus would have made a lousy middle manager!

Most of us can imagine a stern father-figure God, locked in an angry heaven. We can imagine a God who might be tutting at us and with everything lined up and organized and under control. But what about God who was caught up in the hectic business of life? A God who accepted contingency? A God who seemed a bit of a mystery and perhaps even a mess to his followers?

As Jesus rode into Jerusalem on a donkey (Matt. 21:1–11), he was as far from being a world-leader figure as imaginable. It is true that he was fulfilling prophecy (Zech. 9:9), but one man and a donkey must not have looked that grand, especially compared to the militaristic parade going on at the same time from the Romans. The temptation must have been to laugh at his puny preparations and entourage. It would be as though a clown with flappy shoes and a bright red nose had somehow come out on top. And yet, the great anti-manager and anti-despot had the last laugh.

I want to have the last laugh in all my randomness and chaos.

And what about the wonder of the incarnated world?

I cling to the incarnation because it speaks to me of a kind of wonder at the heart of everyday life and everyday people.

We are creatures made and sustained by God (Col. 1:16; Heb. 1:3). We have imagination, compassion and a will to find out more about why we are here. If we just take a minute, we might realize that so many of the things around us are nearly miraculous – we live in such an age.

I live near Heathrow Airport in London. I always have. I no longer hear the planes as they follow their flightpath home. I have been hearing them for nearly sixty years and so they no longer register with me. But occasionally I look up and see the vapour trails and I am filled with wonder.

We barely recognize that our fellow humans are travelling at unimaginable speeds in metal tubes. These tubes have engines and flaps and wings and allow us to go to places we could hardly imagine. Our forebears would have seen us as virtual gods if they had see an aircraft in flight. They would have seen us as wizards who had overcome the laws of nature.

But we live in a world of wonders – wonders created by regular people who have used their minds and vision to carry us forward.

For me, flying is still a thing of wonder. Sometimes while in the air we look down, and in that looking down and around we catch a glimpse of the world we live in. Somehow flying gives us a kind of magic.

Yes, there are wars everywhere, poverty, starvation and injustice. Sometimes we despair and wonder what on earth we are doing to our wonderful world. We wonder if there will ever be a time of peace and justice. We wonder if the Covid-19 pandemic will ever be over. Perhaps we are reminded of the sin within us that fuels so many of the problems. They usually start with us.

But there is so much of our world that helps us to escape some of its gravity – and not just flying. I grew up when we used typewriters, didn't have mobile phones, and there were only a few channels on the

TV. My parents grew up in a world that I would find hard to recognize.

When I get onto an aircraft, I remind myself that being about to turn left on entry, into First Class, is not the real wonder. The wonder is that we can escape the confines of the earth, and fly. I could never be an astronaut, but I could have been a pilot. And now I am a passenger and full of wonder just the same.

If you travel business class on American Airlines you get a special seat and a special space that allows you to set up a kind of mini-office. I imagine business folk pulling down the window shutters, switching on their internet connection and working their way across the Atlantic. I understand that time is money. I used to be a time-is-money kind of person.

But these days I think it might be better to put away the computer and phone and look out of the window at the sky, clouds, stars and the wonderful earth below. Why work when you can be transformed by the near-miracle of sitting in a huge metal bird that can fly without beating its wings?

Study Questions

When we read our Bibles we get a picture of Jesus; not as a proxy, but as a real person. And the more we read, the more extraordinary that picture becomes – and all the more comforting.

What does Jesus' way of running things tell us about God? Do we need to add a certain messiness and unpredictability into our own spiritual lives?

Most of us can imagine a stern father-figure God, locked in an angry heaven. We can imagine a God who might be tutting at us and with everything lined up and organized and under control. But what about God who was caught up in the hectic business of life? A God who accepted contingency? A God who seemed a bit of a mystery and perhaps even a mess to his followers?

Do you imagine God as a stern father? Disapproving? A mystery? Or 'a mess'? How do these terms challenge you? Discuss.

But there is so much of our world that helps us to escape some of its gravity – and not just flying. I grew up when we used typewriters, didn't have mobile phones, and there were only a few channels on the TV. My parents grew up in a world that I would find hard to recognize.

What modern wonders have had an impact on you? What makes you catch your breath? What wonders do you think there might be in the future?

Prayer

Would you help me to see the wonder in the people around me? Help me not to judge others and to see each of them as ultimately precious and amazing. I want to feel the wonder that you feel in the presence of each and every person.
Help me to appreciate the wonders I am surrounded by and to appreciate the people whose work makes it possible. Thank you for the simplicity and complexity of the systems and processes of the world. Thank you, too, for scientists and researchers and engineers.
Help me to be grateful for the extraordinary innovations in this world of ours. Let me not become jaded by what is around me. Let me be happy to be alive in this time, even when there are terrible difficulties, like the Covid-19 pandemic.

12

Creation Sings

Of all the places where we know we might find wonder, creation is the most obvious. Poets have known it for years and the old Jewish poets who gave us the psalms are not shy of declaring it.

Psalm 19 is just one example:

How clearly the sky reveals God's glory!
How plainly it shows what he has done!
Each day announces it to the following day;
each night repeats it to the next.
No speech or words are used,

no sound is heard;
yet their message goes out to all the world
and is heard to the ends of the earth.
God made a home in the sky for the sun;
it comes out in the morning like a happy
bridegroom,
like an athlete eager to run a race.
It starts at one end of the sky
and goes across to the other.
Nothing can hide from its heat.

Psalm 19:1–6, GNT

So many of us experience wonderment in the created world. Of course, you don't need to be a person of faith to revel in our home. But the psalmist tells us that seeing the guiding hand behind it all adds wonder upon wonder.

It is as though creation is singing its own hymn of praise. Creation is a celebration of the goodness of God.

But there is a story behind the story. The natural world is a very cruel world as well – although it looks beautiful. One day I watched a crow attacking a squirrel in my garden. By the time I had got out, the bird had pecked the squirrel to death. It was a gruesome sight. This little drama had been acted out, just outside my window.

In our gardens, daily life-and-death battles are going on all the time. What's more, while we might admire creation, has technology set up a rival camp in terms of an appeal to wonder?

We aren't alone in feeling this. When the railway engine chugged from Stockton to Darlington, the Victorians affirmed a love affair with technology. For such a horseless carriage to move, bellowing smoke like an angry dragon, seemed miraculous. It looked like the future had arrived. There are records of how people were run over and killed by the first horse-less carriages.[1] Clearly, people just could not believe anything could go that fast.

I certainly don't want to set up any false dichot-omy – a battle between technology and creation for the number one spot in wonder. It is simply that we have so many places we might find wonderment.

But the psalmist brings us back to something impor-tant. The creation is calling us to God's tune. Or bet-ter still, the creation sings God's tune. It is as though the creation is so alive with God's creativity that the creation cannot help but reveal his creativity just by being what it is.

We are told that the desire to tell of Jesus is so strong in creation that even the stones would tell his story if they could (Luke 19:40). Creation is full of wonder – what we need to do is take the time to notice.

If creation is calling God's tune, then it is holy. Everything we are surrounded by is bathed with a kind of holiness that we sometimes manage to miss.

Another psalm

It is in the ancient psalms that we get a beautiful and intriguing sense that the world may be much more wonderful than we acknowledge. What if the whole of creation is actually singing a celestial song of thanks to the Creator?

> Praise the LORD from the earth,
> you great sea creatures and all ocean depths,
> lightning and hail, snow and clouds,
> stormy winds that do his bidding,
> you mountains and all hills,
> fruit trees and all cedars,
> wild animals and all cattle,
> small creatures and flying birds,
> kings of the earth and all nations,
> you princes and all rulers on earth,
> young men and women,
> old men and children.

Psalm 148:7–12

What if the whales and dolphins might be praising God? That perhaps is not beyond our imagination. But the psalmist opens up the song. And so, the clouds and the hail and the wind are involved. The creatures we see every day are part of the choir. There is a mystical quality to this in its sense of wholeness and that everything, in the end, connects. As we rattle through our frantic lives, this sudden sense of peace and integration is a welcome relief. Might it help us to stop and take stock and dream a little?

The great fault we so often slip into is to see ourselves as separate from creation. Because we have so many advantages – thumbs, consciousness, the ability to use tools and so on – we miss that we are part of the created order; creatures, like other creatures, alive like the plants and bushes.

Modern apocalyptic movements that forecast the end of the world if we do not treat creation better, understand this. Eco-movements remind us that the earth is more than simply our beautiful home. We are of the earth and we are bound to the whole of creation.

How can we treat the earth with such disdain and so casually? It is a very difficult question. If we truly felt wonder at creation and saw ourselves as part of it, would we even need to be reminded to recycle?

Would the aircraft industry end overnight? Would we turn the electric lights off in our homes? Our oceans appear to be full of plastics and we still buy products packed in them.

When we see ourselves as part of creation, then we get a glimpse of the sheer wonder of being alive. It is this sense of deep connection that we see in the life of St Francis, who loved animals. It is the same insight that spurred the Celtic saints to develop friendships with wild animals and rely on them for their well-being and, sometimes, survival. St Cuthbert, the saint of my church, was greatly aided by an eagle that brought him a salmon to eat when he was hungry.[2]

I want to rediscover this wonder, and I wonder how to do it. On the one hand, reminding myself that God is the source of wonder is helpful. Imagining that he made creation also helps.

We might discard our rubbish and act as though the world is of no consequence. But God has promised that at the end of time the new order will be established here on this precious earth – restored to its true beauty, as all things are made 'new' (Rev. 21:5).

At the heart of wonder is seeing things anew. There is an astonishment to wonder. If we simply notice something, then we are full of wonder.

How might we gain a new love of creation? One of the things that helped me begin to see creation anew was a thought. Why is creation so beautiful? What purpose does that beauty serve? It could just as well be monochrome and simply functional. The world, the creation, is unnecessarily beautiful. I owe it to both God and the world around me to at least open myself to the possibility of being surprised by creation and challenge myself always to see it anew and wonder what I might learn from it.

Perhaps the problem is that I have been looking for big set-piece examples of wonder. Perhaps I might need to lower my eyes and see what is actually around me.

Maybe beauty is not always found in the grand sweep of a sublime landscape or a beautiful sunset. Perhaps we should consider more the scale and depth of the wonder of the world around us – as though a single grain of sand might be all we needed in order to know that we live among wonderment.

The key to wonderment isn't a great view or a stirring vista. These things are amazing, but they wear off. Perhaps real wonderment kicks in when we see that we ourselves are

> Real wonderment kicks in when we see that we ourselves are intrinsically bound to creation.

intrinsically bound to creation. We are not separate from creation. And then we begin to get a sense that if we are part of creation, then every single one of us has something to add. If we weren't here the world would be worse – and the story of creation incomplete.

Study Questions

I certainly don't want to set up any false dichotomy – a battle between technology and creation for the number one spot in wonder. It is simply that we have so many places we might find wonderment.

Where do you find wonder most often?

Creation is full of wonder – what we need to do is take the time to notice.

How can you take time to notice, today?

Maybe beauty is not always found in the grand sweep of a sublime landscape or a beautiful sunset. Perhaps we should consider more the scale and depth of the wonder of the world around us – as though a single grain of sand might be all we needed in order to know that we live among wonderment.

Do you agree?

Prayer

*Open us to the wonder of your creation, dear
Lord. Help us to see your hand at work in all that
surrounds us. Fill us with such wonder that each
day we are struck by the beauty and creativity at
work in our home planet.*
*If we are jaded, help us with a moment of
revelation. Let us see your handprint in the flowers
and hills and grass, let us see your influence in the
insects and the trees. Open our eyes to creation in
all its wonder and open our ears as well.*
*Creation cries your song aloud. Help us to be singers
in this great choir too.*
*Thank you that we are not separate from creation,
but wondrously part of it as well. So, let us care for
it as we would our most precious friend.*

13

The Meal of Wonder

I was enjoying watching a row of parishioners snaking up to the front of the church for communion. Each took their turn to stand in front of me, put out their hands and politely take the wafer.

Towards the back of the queue was a young family. Their 6-year-old put her hands out and I placed a tiny piece of wafer into them. She ate it and called out to her mum: 'Mmm, yummy.'

It was such a wonderful response that I wondered why more of us don't do it. Rather than saying a reverent 'amen', why not a loud and boisterous 'yummy'?

Early days and beyond

I know that when I was growing up, I didn't really like communion – largely because I was reluctant to be in church and, when there, didn't understand what was going on. And the church was bitterly cold, and no one smiled or spoke to us.

On the odd occasion I went to church as a boy, I always hoped I hadn't chosen a Eucharist service. To be honest, I was very bored in church and I saw the Eucharist as just prolonging the agony.

That same feeling persisted into adulthood. I began to go very, very occasionally to a church in Ealing. I liked being in a church but, when it was a communion week, I wished I had been at home. On the one hand it seemed to take forever and, also, I felt I had no part in it. I was baptized as an infant, but I made no connection between that baptism and this sacrament. And so I offer this chapter with a little hesitancy.

For some, I know, sitting it out as others come up and take the bread and wine can seem isolating and as if they are not part of a mysterious club. It pains me when I am presiding to see a few people left in the pews who do not feel they can, or want to, come forward. I believe in a generous God who wants to offer all the chance to come and eat and drink with him. I wonder if communion is just for the initiated, or does it point to a deeper wonder accessible for all? Most of the wonderments I have investigated in these pages are available to all, but is this an insiders' wonder?

I studied for ordination at a college that was predominantly conservative evangelical. I loved it and my conservative friends are still friends. But I wonder, would it be fair to say that the Eucharist stood a bit behind our Bible studies? I understand why. We tended to see the Eucharist as just what we might have called a memorial – a bringing to mind of the Christ-story which, of course, is a wonderful thing. But I have come to feel that there is more to the Eucharist than this.

So let me try to understand why there is wonder in the Eucharist.

The Eucharist and its scope

Thinking about it now, I often feel more of a connection with the mystery and wonder at communion than I do during the sermon, prayers, or worship. Sometimes when I have led a service, I get an awful feeling that the only truly holy moment was the Eucharist – but every preacher always feels they fail.

Dom Gregory Dix was an Anglican priest and monk. He was much interested in liturgy and was a key thinker on liturgical reforms in the church before he died at a very young age.

It was a passage from Gregory Dix's book, *The Shape of the Liturgy*, which helped me to understand one of the reasons why the Eucharist has become for me a source of revelation and wonder. He wrote of how, throughout history and all around the world, the faithful – priests and people – have obeyed the command of Jesus to eat and drink, 'in remembrance' of him (Luke 22:19). There is something universal about the Eucharist.

Dix points out the reach of communion – the way it stands at different times of life, different circumstances and in different places. It is a kind of sacred language, a sacred place open to the people of God. Timothy Radcliffe pointed out to me something of this – the importance of where and how we celebrate the Eucharist:

> I have most often experienced the wonder of the liturgy in places of desolation. In Rwanda, when the country was building up to the genocide, after journeying all day and witnessing the effects of the violence that had already occurred, and sensing what was to come, I experienced the

astonishing gift of the Eucharist, of the one who, faced only with apparent failure and disaster, could say, 'This is my body given for you'.[1] Similarly in Syria, not four miles from the front line with Daesh, the words of consecration, of utter gift, are filled with wonder. They are words of utter creativity, of the God who made everything *ex nihilo*, faced with raw destruction and negativity.[2]

I sometimes wonder if the Eucharist has actually saved the church. It is, in some ways, the one constant of its practise and in times of disagreement, near-warfare and conflict, the breaking of bread has always been there.

Plus, the words of the Eucharist remind us in the same way each time of the story we proclaim. What other words could we need? In my charismatic church we were always waiting on the Spirit to help us to find the right words – the right words of prayer, comfort, prophecy, and to help us to extemporize during worship. We were also waiting upon the Lord to give us the gift of tongues.[3]

Of course, none of this is wrong in the slightest. More than that, it is beautiful and right.

But in our insistence on finding new words, we sometimes miss the sheer wonder of the old ones

and the old established sacred moments. As we go
through the Eucharist, we go on a journey that takes
us through some of the key teachings of the church.

It begins and ends with thankfulness

The Gospel of Mark explains:

> Then [Jesus] took a cup, and when he had given
> thanks, he gave it to them, and they all drank
> from it. 'This is my blood of the covenant, which
> is poured out for many,' he said to them.
>
> Mark 14:23,24

The Gospels reveal Jesus to be
a thankful person. Underlying
his teaching and his ministry is
a deep thankfulness to God.

> The Gospels
> reveal Jesus to
> be a thankful
> person.

In the familiar passage from Mark's Gospel, the
story of the Last Supper, Jesus takes the bread and
the wine and gives thanks. Giving thanks to God was
as natural as breathing to him, but in this moment,
Jesus' thanksgiving is particularly remarkable. During
the supper, Jesus is concerned that one of the disciples, one of his friends, will soon betray him. He
would also, no doubt, have spent much of the meal
contemplating his coming, inevitable, death. Here is
a remarkable thankfulness, born of a thankful life.

Jesus' prayer of thanks at the Last Supper was one of the earliest prayers of the infant church. And still we continue to do this in every church, all over the world – to 'do this in remembrance' of him (Luke 22:19; 1 Cor. 11:24).

And this prayer, in whatever language it is prayed, is 'Eucharist': simply the Greek word for 'thanksgiving'. It takes us back to the thankfulness of Jesus. We give thanks. Yet the depth of this prayer lies in the fact that, when we pray it, we are not just giving thanks for food and drink. Yes, in one prayer of thanks we have a snapshot of the history of our salvation: the awesome wonder of God's love.

When we give thanks for the body of Christ, we give thanks, not only for the embodiment of the Word (John 1:14), but also for the Word come as 'food'. We acknowledge that Christ himself is present with us: present not only in the sacrament of Holy Communion, but also in the feeding of the hungry and the care of the poor. Christ giving of himself in acts of faith and love. Christ present where love is offered, but Christ also made present in love received; Christ in the cared for as well as the carer.

Bishop Michael Colclough tells me:

I once heard the story told of a Roman Catholic priest working in Peru. The people were very poor.

He noticed a woman come to Mass who he knew had not been to confession. After the service she came to him in tears and apologized for not having first made her confession. She told him that she had come into the church, and although she knew she was not worthy, still, when she saw the bread in the hands of the priest, hunger overwhelmed her. She had just needed the tiny piece of bread. The priest, humbled by this encounter, reflected on the practical giving of the body of Christ, and how Christ had physically, as well as spiritually, fed the starving woman. Her faith – and her need – had nourished the priest's faith. A reminder, too, that we need this food for the journey of our pilgrimage: food that is both a pointer and a foretaste of the Heavenly Banquet to which we are called. How hungry am I – are you – for that food?[4]

In the bread and wine that we offer, in the body and blood that we share, we have the focus for all our thanksgiving. Creation, the incarnation, the passion and resurrection, the church of which we are members, and the forgiveness of our sins. Day by day, week by week, we take, break and share together this mystery as we give thanks in the Eucharist. And, of course, all of this is too great for us to grasp in one go, and we can never be thankful enough. There is always more for which we can give thanks to God – even when we find ourselves, like Jesus at the Last Supper, in the midst of crisis.

That is why, week by week, we return to those words of Christ. Each time we hear them, each time we hold in our hand the tiny piece of bread, or taste the sip of wine, each time is a gospel moment when something new can strike us afresh, something for which we can give thanks: the taste of food, the fellowship with others, the forgiveness for our sins, the mystery of Christmas, the salvation of Good Friday, the new life and hope of Easter. All this is there as we meet the Eucharistic Christ.

'Do this in remembrance of me' (Luke 22:19). When we hear those words of Jesus, we do well not to miss the wonder and holiness of that moment. For in the words of *The Book of Common Prayer*:

> The Body of our Lord Jesus Christ, which was given for thee, preserve thy body and soul unto everlasting life: Take and eat this in remembrance that Christ died for thee, and feed on him in thy heart by faith with thanksgiving.
>
> *The Book of Common Prayer*.
> Reproduced with permission of Cambridge
> University Press through PLSclear.[5]

But it was talking to a friend and local parish priest that helped me to really nail my understanding of why the Eucharist is a place of wonder. Reverend Lyndon North explained that while teaching Bible studies to a large group of students he suddenly realised that the Eucharist is central to evangelism: 'For whenever you eat this bread and drink this cup, you proclaim the Lord's death until he comes' (1 Cor. 11:26).

It is the place where people have an encounter with the risen Lord and experience his grace and love.[6]

Study Questions

I know that when I was growing up, I didn't really like communion – largely because I was reluctant to be in church and, when there, didn't understand what was going on. And the church was bitterly cold, and no one smiled or spoke to us.

How has your understanding of communion developed over the years?

Dix points out the reach of communion – the way it stands at different times of life, different circumstances and in different places. It is a kind of sacred language, a sacred place open to the people of God.

Discuss.

In the bread and wine that we offer, in the body and blood that we share, we have the focus for all our thanksgiving. Creation, the incarnation, the passion and resurrection, the church of which we are members, and the forgiveness of our sins.

Discuss.

Prayer

Help us to understand the deep significance and wonder of the Eucharist, whatever tradition we come from. Let us honour the traditions of others and deepen our understanding of this sacrament. We thank you for every Eucharistic service that has ever been, and especially for those that have taken place in times of fear and trouble.
We pray for those who celebrate the Eucharist today in places where it is perilous to do so. Help us to encounter you in this holy space.

14

Art in a Vacuum

Can we accept that wonder is a way of breaking us free from the imprisonment of the self; of helping us to connect with the world and each other in new ways? Wonder is an antidote to loneliness, to self-absorption and the dead hand of seeing things as we have always seen them. It is a gateway to the God of wonderment.

If this is so, then we explorers after wonder must surely take at least a glance at art and its claims and powers, to see what wonderment we can find there. I ask Timothy Radcliffe about the powerful relationship between wonder and art. He tells me that art is a barrier against literalistic ways of seeing the world and, as such, is an attempt to reclaim a poetic imagination at the heart of life.

> I would say that human culture is essentially poetic. Humans are always hungering for a plenitude of meaning which is beyond our full grasp. We reach out in poetry, but also through novels, painting, films, etc. Wonderment is at the essence of our humanity.

I am in Brussels visiting my favourite conceptual artist. Pieter Laurens Mol uses sculpture and photography. His themes are tied up with the wonder of science and its relation to religion. He sees art as a way of mediating between the two – of creating a new space. He's had a troubled relation with religion. As a boy he was sent to a Catholic boarding school run by monks. 'It was sometimes cruel and I was lonely,' he tells me.

His study is neat in the extreme. We could be in the presence of an architect, which isn't that surprising, as his father was an architect.

What has drawn me to Pieter's work over the years is that so much of it seems to be about escaping gravity and reaching for wonder. He doesn't shy away from the flip side, either. His works depicting depression and defeat are poignant, to say the least. But the depression and defeat aren't the end of the story.

But in some ways Pieter is a kid at heart – his art is peppered with rockets, and vapour trails from aircraft and moonlight. Pieter's work holds in tension both the wonderment and escape, and the depths of depression.

Figure 1   *Blue Defeat* © Pieter Laurens Mol

Can you have one without the other? Pieter's *Blue Defeat* (reproduced in greyscale at Figure 1) seems to say that there is only one trajectory. The artist fallen like a squashed fly. But as I have found out, wonderment is the close companion of the other side of human experience. We feel wonder all the more keenly when we know how low it is possible to go.

Perhaps that's why Pieter's work so often features the planet Saturn with its long association with melancholy. When we escape the bounds of earth and aim for freedom, the dread that we might be pulled back down or be on a fool's errand must strike any thinking person.

He tells me:

> I am Dutch and we Dutch have a reputation for being level and perhaps given to gloominess. The physical conditions of the Netherlands have had an influence on all Dutch artists. The weather is gloomy. There is constantly damp in the air. We do not have the azure skies of California. But if you look at the work of the Dutch masters, you would think otherwise. For them, the skies are blue and there is that incredible, magical Dutch light – with crispy clouds and beautiful skies. Just

look at Vermeer. But the truth is, they made it all up. That isn't what it is like here. They wanted to create a world that was lively, optimistic and wonderful.

The Dutch masters wanted to hint at wonder and to manipulate the world, but perhaps that is what art is for.

Where do we get to the crux, we wonder-seekers? Pieter tells me a story about how he wanted to solve all of the problems of art, and life. He wondered if the secret of finding wonder was to create a place of nothingness where it could then grow. If you could clear away life's complications, overcoming all conflicts, then perhaps something that explained everything might emerge.

> When I was 18, I was very caught up in the adventure of art. I wanted to find a place that could get rid of all dualisms – a place that was whole and of itself. In the mid-sixties I was very influenced by Yves Klein. In the year 1958 he had put on an exhibition called *'Le Vide'* [The Void]. It was an empty gallery space, nothing to see – no art, really, nothing, just space. He was a mystic. I became obsessed with the idea of creating an absolute space and to overcome all complexity.

A place of wonder where everything connected without distraction.

I began to wonder if I could solve all the problems of art by making a space like this. And it occurred to me that I should make a place of nothingness where soul and spirit should meet. I decided to create a small glass sphere. I would have all the air sucked out of it and I would then carry it around. It was as though I would be walking around with the answer to all of art's problems – with the solution, a clear space.

I was probably influenced by Torricelli, who invented the barometer. He used an 'absence of air' instead of a true vacuum. But then I began to be tortured by this idea. Because in our material world what we call a vacuum is never really a place with nothing in it. There is always something there – even if it is an invisible radiation still unknown to us. So, in an absolute sense, nothing doesn't exist, because there always might be something. I was disappointed, I suppose. But the rest of my career has been about finding, creating and sharing that place of true wonderment. I have been looking for a positive alternative to the vacuum all my life.[1]

Pieter's quest may have failed, but he is onto something. The vacuum, the call of nothingness, will never be the answer. Still, the desire to find a place where things can seem whole is a noble one. But then the vacuum is in one sense never empty of everything, or at least empty of the possibility of containing something.

Art may be a reflector of wonder and a creator of a space for wonderment. It helps us to see the world anew and its connections and mysteries. But perhaps without a different focus then it will always be like that vacuum carried around as part of an experiment with nothingness. How do we reach outwards to something or someone that might help us live a life of more purpose and constant wonder that feels more like space-dancing than vacuum-making?

> Art may be a reflector of wonder and a creator of a space for wonderment.

Therefore Jesus said again, 'Very truly I tell you, I am the gate for the sheep. All who have come before me are thieves and robbers, but the sheep have not listened to them. I am the gate; whoever enters through me will be saved. They will come in and go out, and find pasture. The thief comes only to steal and kill and destroy; I have come that they may have life, and have it to the full.'

John 10:7–10

I am not unaware of the voices that say a dedication to wonderment might be a selfish pleasure – a call to withdraw from the world into a world of sensation. But we can't really sustain this when we see the supercharged life that Christ seems to be calling us into.

Christ's famous words don't skirt round the problem. We are all surrounded by thieves and robbers. We can all fall off the path and be waylaid – by temptation, by harmful world views, by the presence of intentional evil. But Christ's call is that with him around we can live a life that is marked by a kind of spiritual, emotional and practical abundance that will transform everything.

I think that wonderment is part of that equation because it helps us to see that we aren't trapped in ourselves and that there is something surprising, beautiful and amazing at the heart of the messy business of being alive. Wonderment is a gift. It is a sudden understanding or perception that the life lived to the full is possible.

Study Questions

Wonder is an antidote to loneliness, to self-absorption and the dead hand of seeing things as we have always seen them. It is a gateway to the God of wonderment.

Do you agree? Why? Or why not?

Art may be a reflector of wonder and a creator of a space for wonderment. It helps us to see the world anew and its connections and mysteries. But perhaps without a different focus then it will always be like that vacuum carried around as part of an experiment with nothingness.

Discuss.

I think that wonderment is part of that equation because it helps us to see that we aren't trapped in ourselves and that there is something surprising, beautiful and amazing at the heart of the messy business of being alive. Wonderment is a gift. It is a sudden understanding or perception that the life lived to the full is possible.

Discuss.

Prayer

Lord, help us to understand the truth that there is always something rather than nothing; help us to be explorers of that something. Bless the artists and authors and poets who risk themselves to express so much about the human condition.

15

The Photographer and the Café

George Miles is a photographer and lecturer who has discovered the mighty power of wonder. I meet him in a café in north London and we pore over his photos as we drink coffee. It's his collection[1] on Matlock Bath in Derbyshire that grabs my attention – where photos of nature and others of rundown cafés and garages stand next to each other.

George explains that Matlock Bath is local to where he grew up. It's an odd place – a seaside town without the seaside. Whatever it's like now, it's got an interesting history. Byron stayed there, and Ruskin, in its glory days. It was where Thomas Cook offered some of the first package holidays.

With the Industrial Revolution and the coming of the railways it became a leisure destination for the urban working class. There were penny arcades and dance halls.

It has been a place that has known dancing and healing and all manner of human occupation.

George began a labour of love. Each Monday for three years he photographed Matlock Bath. It was no tiny modern digital camera. Instead, it was a huge old plate camera – bad for the back, I'm sure. But the weight of the camera meant that George had to slow down and take things in – let the place speak to him. George tells me:

> I discovered myself as I took those pictures. I wanted to show what man had done to nature. But then I got to break out of these constraints and take pictures of nature too. The place began to work on me.

It was a wonderment located in the everyday places – the neglected places.

What George discovered was nothing less than wonderment. It was a wonderment located in the everyday places – the neglected places.

I began to have this sense of awe. It wasn't rational at all . . . I began to see beauty was there in
places I didn't expect it – in the piece of rubbish
lodged in a tree, in garages and cafés as well as
the woodlands.

The nature was wonderful, but so were the other
places. And it's here that we see a real breakthrough.
George explains that we want to see a version of
flawless nature – the traditional picture. But not far
from every site of natural beauty is a car park, or
a road, or a rubbish bin. What about those places?
If we appreciated that nature is compromised, and
lived with these imperfections, then we might stop
idolizing it, and see wonder everywhere. 'Then we
might care for it more,' George says.

But what of the three-year project?

I see it as a way of saying thank you. I guess you
could describe that as a kind of prayer. One of the
photos is of a cottage. I kept going back and it wasn't
quite ready for me. Each time there was a red Land
Rover outside, and it would have made a very kitsch
photo. One day, years after I started, I got to the cottage and the Land Rover was gone, replaced by an
old Peugeot 106 GTI with a tyre off and up on a car
jack. I felt it would be rude of me not to take what
was then the picture the place needed.

George explains that he began to realize there were so many coincidences happening as he came back week after week. These coincidences delivered pictures over and again.

> I began to wonder if these moments of wonder are happening all the time and what we have to do is change our perception – to allow wonder to meet us halfway. In a way it's all about light. When the light catches a piece of rubbish stuck in a tree trunk then it becomes something more than rubbish – it alters the way we see it. Photography is about light.[2]

Figure 2 **'Jay Cees' Café: North Parade'** © George Miles

And the café? One of the great pictures in George's book is called 'Jay Cees' Café: North Parade'. (See Figure 2.) It features a Formica-style table with four chairs and some condiments. It is awash with browns and even features a bottle of brown sauce. But the more we look at this desolate scene, something grabs us. Is it the serenity of the place, or the expectancy that the chairs may be filled? Does it help us to stop and value neglected places? It is a place of surprising harmony – the browns are beautiful.

What seemed prosaic was in fact alive with the kind of wonderous possibilities usually reserved for a cathedral. That's it – the old-style café is an unexpected chapel, a place pregnant with awe and wonder. An unexpected 'thin' place in the midst of all our activity.

Study Questions

I began to have this sense of awe. It wasn't rational at all . . . I began to see beauty was there in places I didn't expect it – in the piece of rubbish lodged in a tree, in garages and cafés as well as the woodlands.

How do you respond to this?

But the more we look at this desolate scene, something grabs us. Is it the serenity of the place, or the expectancy that the chairs may be filled? Does it help us to stop and value neglected places? It is a place of surprising harmony – the browns are beautiful.

And how do you respond to this?

Prayer

So often we walk past examples of your wonder in the everyday. Open our eyes to holy encounters in these places. Your wonder is all around us – in cafés, in nature, in places that look scruffy and unloved. Help us to take our time and be attentive. Can we be surprised by God in the everyday? We do hope so. Let us be distracted enough to take notice, and curious enough to wonder whether wonder might strike us and transform us in the midst of our normal lives.

16

Living the Wonderful Life

I have searched for wonder and spoken to people who might help me to uncover it. There have been artists and photographers and parents. The evidence seems to suggest that wonder is out there and regularly felt by most of us – but that we sometimes fail to know what to do with it. Perhaps we struggle with vocabulary and world view to incorporate wonder as a way of being and not just as a random experience.

But time and again it is an understanding of God as the heart of wonderment that has helped people to see it more as a way of life than simply a passing emotion.

The truth is that I have been searching after wonder since my earliest days.

Perhaps the Old English warriors as they set up camp in what is now Northolt felt *wundor* – that there was something marvellous or astonishing in this place. If they did, then they'd be hard-pushed to find its modern incarnation all that marvellous.

One of the reasons that I cling to the possibility of wonderment goes right back to the roots of my childhood. I grew up in the far suburbs, as far west as you can go, in London.

Our house was in a street that was probably named as a result of a joke among the planners and local council. We lived in Lilliput Avenue, the land of the little people.[1] I guess there would never be a Lilliput Avenue in Mayfair or Chelsea. I never found the street name odd until I went to university and many of my new friends found it funny.

Even when I was growing up, Northolt had a problem with roads. These days my old family house is a stone's throw from the eight-lane Western Avenue. Cars thunder by day and night into London and back to the Midlands and beyond. We are simply a place that people drive through on the way to somewhere else.

Even as boy, the roads seemed to be everywhere. Our house was just past the major roundabout and the pub that is now a 24-hour McDonalds. Like many suburban children, I had a strong sense that life was to be had elsewhere.

In the grey and drabness of Northolt, I often wondered where the wonder was. I think my parents shared some of this. At every opportunity we hopped into the car and headed out to the country for a day trip. We always wanted to be somewhere else. We had the sense that wonder was just beyond the horizon.

It was only with my conversion much later in life that I began to have a hope that wonder was more than just the odd experience and might be a way of life. Perhaps the horizon is an illusion. Wonder is everywhere.

The image of Edward White hangs over this book. The first US astronaut to do a space-walk decided to make it a space-ballet. So greatly was he enraptured that he nearly died from lack of oxygen. Back on earth, he shared the nugget of his experience. I come back to his gracious space-ballet as an image of a life of wonderment.

God as the creator of wonder

John V. Taylor, in his classic *The Go-Between God*,[2] has strong insights into the very nature of wonder and just why God might be involved in it all. He points out that people are having experiences of wonder all the time. These are not necessarily religious in any way, but they are driven by the work of the Holy Spirit – they are the spirit of annunciation. The Holy Spirit is permanently announcing wonderment to us and connecting us to its source.

When we are infants, we don't perceive any difference between ourselves and the other objects and people around us. As we grow up, we get a distinct idea of 'I' and 'other'. Wonderment comes when that division between 'I' and 'other' is broken down and we allow ourselves to somehow communicate or join with the world around us.

Wonderment is when we are present to the world around us. The glorious mountain we see ceases to be an object and becomes a subject. It exists and says something to us. In this way we see things with new eyes.

Taylor argues that this communication, this odd, wondrous sense of being part of something bigger than ourselves, is the work of the Go-Between

God. The Holy Spirit, he says, opens and facilitates this pattern of communication. It is the Holy Spirit that develops this sense of communication. It is this place in which new truth and new awareness grows.

No need to chase wonder

There is a danger to chasing wonder as a kind of enchantment, as an escape from life. There is a danger of privatizing it – a personal pursuit of the ecstatic or transcendental. Wonder isn't bewitchment; at least, it shouldn't be.

Artist Pieter Laurens Mol tells me: 'It is great to be talented and gifted and to experience joy and wonder and beauty. But wonder has to be shared if it is to mean anything at all. There is no delight in it if we don't find ways of sharing it – that's what artists do; they share wonder and help us to see it together.'[3]

Perhaps this is why artists seem to have been so interested in it.

There is an old Benedictine prayer[4] which shows how wonderment is the gateway to a more purposeful life. Wonder is the fuel and energy that sends us out. If wonder is a spiritual rocket fuel, then we had better be prepared for it to spur us into a new way of life.

The prayer has it that wonder is an opening of our eyes and a spur to sharing our many blessings with those around us. Wonder is allied with generosity – shown practically and with a generosity of spirit. In a way this takes us

> Wonder is allied with generosity – shown practically and with a generosity of spirit.

back to that image of the saints as people who leave a trail of light. One way of finding wonderment is to find an everyday saint and be part of what they are doing. Wonder is closer and more available than we think.

Wonderment asks us to think again and look again. To see the creation anew, and our loved ones and our communities as well. It calls us to see ourselves as part of a dramatic big story that both puts our lives into perspective, without us at the centre of everything, but also as precious, awesome creatures sharing our world with others. Perhaps we are also called to see wonderment in the day-to-day business of life.

For me, my sense of wonder has only grown as I have wondered about the nature of God. Paul on the road to Damascus (Acts 9) suddenly realized that God was close and that life was simpler than he thought. A God who finds us, and everyone else, precious – now, that's a life-changer.

This morning on the radio[5] I heard that a snail has more than 10,000 teeth. When I heard this, I laughed out loud. I am still smiling as I write this. Who would have thought it! How does my friend the snail fit them into that tiny mouth? It has made my day. It makes me want to hunt out a snail in my back garden and spend some time looking at it and wondering what it feels like to have all those teeth.

George Miles, my photographer friend, found wonder in a broken-down and deserted café in an ordinary town. His pictures reclaim a kind of everyday, even blighted, wonder. If we weren't in a rush, we might experience just such awe ourselves.

In my conversation with Timothy Radcliffe, I asked him, what might a life and a church filled with wonder actually look like? How might it transform the way we live life and faith? He answered:

> Growing in wonderment implies a way of life which is not rapacious, and non-violent. Sexual abuse represents the polar opposite from such a way of being. It touches how one regards wealth. In St Francis of Assisi one sees the model of how another way of being is needed. His simplicity of life opens him to the glory.[6]

Is wonder a luxury?

As I write this, a warning bell is sounding. Wonder is OK, but what if you are working as, say, a tyre-fitter or a machinist and a job is there to be done? There is money to be earned and the business of life to be got through.

Isn't it a luxury? If we start going all out for wonder, might we lose a hold on the very practical tasks we have to do? Life is hard and we have to get through much of it with gritted teeth. It sounds good to rediscover a childlike wonder, but faced with some of the realities people face that seems a big ask. As my father was man-handling a carpet into a house to start a job, not sure if his knee would hold out, wonderment might have seemed in the far distance.

If you are on a dinghy that might sink at any moment and you are paddling for your life to start again away from a war-torn place – where is wonder then? I do not want to be trite.

But what I can say is that sometimes in my very lowest and perilous times, I have had an odd sense of something that I now call 'God whispering his presence'.

So, what does the wonder-filled life look like? Bishop Michael Colclough told me this:

> When you have confidence in God – deep con-
> fidence in him – then it is liberating and you

don't need to be frightened of others and their reactions. You can be yourself. Think about when God says of Jesus when he is baptized: 'This is my [beloved] . . . with him I am well pleased.'[7] You cannot say 'I am well pleased' without a smile on your face. That reminds us of the divine smile when God looks at us. God is delighted in us. That means that, even if we are going through a hard time, then there is a bedrock of happiness in our lives. And that means a propensity to joy.[8]

The wonder-filled life

When I became a Christian, I read and re-read the Gospel of John. As I read it again, I see that John's gospel is a story of the wonderment of the Christ and it reads, to me, as a kind of recipe or tantalizing rumour of what it is to live a life filled with wonder, rather than as a spiritual thrill-seeker. It covers deep and abiding themes and dilemmas – what it is to love and the riskiness of loving others, the power and wonder of friendship, and hope in the darkest time where it seems that evil will win.

John was an old man when he wrote his gospel. Perhaps he was in exile. He had a lifetime to think back to those few years that he spent with his friend who turned out to be God.

Given that Jesus had entrusted his mother to John's care, perhaps they had years talking about the time when God was with us.

Can we be diverted?

I am the kind of person who tends to want to get a journey over as quickly as possible. I can almost hear me as a boy pestering my parents with, 'Are we nearly there yet?' As an adult, that mentality showed itself as what we might call being 'goal-focused'. I became a person who made lists of the things I needed to do for the day ahead. I had goals.

But now I see the world a different way around. I welcome being diverted and my list days are long gone. My encounter with the wonder of God has somehow made me much more open to being diverted.

Jesus was the master of being diverted. He never seemed in a hurry. It was as though he managed to be fully present in each moment and open to where life would take him next.

At the start of John's gospel, Jesus is gathering his inner ring of followers. He doesn't have a person spec, or a psychological profile. Instead, he recruits by simply wandering around and seeing what happens. His followers are hardworking people – some of them fishermen. They have things to do and a schedule to keep.

Jesus diverts them and simply says, 'Come and see' (John 1:39, GNT). He comes across two people and asks the most diverting question: 'What are you looking for?' (John 1:38, GNT). It is a question very relevant to our lost world. The two go to Jesus' home and become followers.

A gateway to the wonder-filled life is to be open to being diverted and to be open to the possibility of being surprised. Are we ready for the unexpected? Can we ever be ready?

George Miles tells me that he tells his students not to be too fixed. If they spot a crisp packet on the way to doing a portrait, then they should allow themselves the possibility that a picture of the crisp packet might be the picture that they *should* take.

In the first chapter of John's gospel, Jesus hints that life with him is going to be about the unexpected. Nathanael has an inkling that Jesus is something truly special. I believe Jesus finds his comment amusing.

> Very truly I tell you, you will see 'heaven open, and the angels of God ascending and descending on' the Son of Man.
>
> John 1:51

Can we escape ourselves?

We can be a great burden to ourselves. We are rooted in time and place; of course we are. But we long to sometimes escape and get a different perspective – to be lost in the moment we are in. Wonder might be just part of a road to healing. It is a great burden to feel we always have to take control of our lives and make the most of ourselves. But what about a sense of freedom that allows us to escape some of our bonds? Perhaps Christ's words in Matthew 10:39 are a clue:

> Whoever finds their life will lose it, and whoever loses their life for my sake will find it.

Are we eternally grateful?

These days, I find myself more and more grateful. When I list the things I am grateful for, most of them come back somehow to God. I am grateful that I am still alive. I am grateful for the people around me. I am grateful for my pets and the creation that I am part of. I am grateful that I had an education and that I have had an interesting life.

My faith adds a dimension to wonderment that I never thought I could feel. I had so many years when

I suffered from depression. Anyone who has had that condition knows the feeling of waking up and knowing that the day is only going in one direction.

Gratitude was at the heart of God-on-earth's life. He was thankful for his followers (although they exasperated him), he was thankful to his Father in heaven. He wondered why those he healed did not come back to say thank you (Luke 17:17,18).

An incident on the Apollo 11 mission to the moon encapsulates the grateful life and its dance with wonderment. I have sometimes written that the problem with Neil Armstrong was that he was no poet. He was prosaic and a reluctant commentator on the wonder he experienced. Had he captured some of the experience in words, then perhaps we would still be flying to the moon today, inspired by him. But I now question whether I am wrong. Armstrong had a particular job – to get the landing craft down safely and to get the team home. Just before the landing on the moon, he realized that something was going wrong. The spacecraft was travelling too quickly and disaster was at hand. The flimsy computing power of the mission was letting them down. Armstrong took decisive action. He navigated manually and the day was saved. If he had been a poet and not a scientist and military man, the moon landing would have ended in disaster, perhaps.

Sometimes we need to take our eyes off the wonderment outside the window and concentrate on the small wonder of human ingenuity and practicality.

Something else prompts us to engage with wonder. Buzz Aldrin may have been the second man on the moon, but he was also the first man to celebrate communion in space. He took with him a small fragment of blessed bread and wine and paused to take the sacrament. He also encouraged an audience of many, many millions to also pause and be grateful.

As the world paused and reflected on wonder and the eerie majesty of space and human ingenuity of science, we saw perhaps the most natural response to wonderment – to say thank you to the God who is the sustainer of everything (Col. 1:16; Heb. 1:3).

Is our life about service and sacrifice?

Again, in John's gospel, Christ spells out the cost of serving others (6:53–9). His ministry, which at first seemed almost carefree, full of one wonderment after another, comes to a grinding halt. Those who were there just soaking up his healings are confronted with an inconvenient truth. Preaching in the synagogue in Capernaum, Christ tells those who are listening that at some point they will need to 'eat the flesh' and 'drink [the] blood' of the Son of Man. It is a line that confused many and led to problems for the early church – the Roman authorities wondered if the Christ-sect were cannibals.

But the implication is that we are called also to put others first, as Christ himself was about to do with his own body and blood.

When we experience wonder and we live it out, then it is an engine, a fuel that helps us to engage with the world and not retreat from it. Wonder is a powerful driver to encourage us to care for others.

There is a telling moment. Christ's followers have discovered the empty tomb and that their friend has been raised from the dead. He ascends back to heaven. Their response is to gaze up to the sky in wonderment. But angels correct them – why were they looking up there for him (Acts 1:11)? The call, instead, is to get on with the work. That work is to look with new eyes on the poor, the hungry, the imprisoned and the destitute. They are to find Christ incarnate in each other, in their neighbours and in the suffering world.

Wonder leads to reordering of priorities and the knowledge that accumulating wealth, status, or any of the other temptations of the world will never really be enough.

Christ lives this out – not least when he scandalizes his followers by washing their feet (John 13:5–7). If we accept that Christ is God, then what does this action say to us? It is wonderful beyond wonderful and calls us to a new sense of purpose.

Do we see ourselves as part of a bigger story?

If wonder is not just an experience but a way of being, then it has a bigger story to tell than we thought. Wonder whispers to us that we are both less significant than we think (that we aren't the centre of the universe) and also part of a much bigger story.

We hear about this new narrative at the very start of John's gospel:

> In the beginning was the Word, and the Word was with God, and the Word was God. He was with God in the beginning. Through him all things were made . . .

> John 1:1–3

If this is true, and at least for me it was not a stretch to believe it, then the everyday becomes a matter of wonderment. When we see a beautiful bird in our garden, or glance at the heavens, then we see them both linked to a story of creation that we are part of as well. We are not a cosmic accident, and that is a truly awesome thought. Creation was a purposeful action by God.

But creation is, of course, only part of the Christian narrative. The picture of God as one of us, and then suffering and dying for and with us, adds dignity to even the humblest life. When we add the ultimate triumph of love, then we would be hard-hearted indeed not to see ourselves in a new way, and those we share the planet with.

Can we embrace a new way of seeing and being?

Exposure to the Christ of the Gospels warps 'reality'. He calls us back to things we had forgotten and grown out of. Perhaps one of the most astounding claims is that God is gentle, friendly and on our side.

> I no longer call you servants, because a servant does not know his master's business. Instead, I have called you friends, for everything that I learned from my Father I have made known to you.
>
> John 15:15

Now, to some this might sound fanciful. Given the vastness of the galaxies, the infinity of space and the insignificance of a single life, how could there be a

God who might be so personal? But many millions of people over the generations can attest to an odd sense that God is not the angry dictator in a cold heaven that he is often portrayed as.

Whatever the case, wonder calls us out of ourselves to engage with the source of that wonder, and at the very least, to ask some profound questions about why we are here and what our lives mean. If we embrace the Christian story of wonder, then it is an encouragement, not so much to evangelize, as to enjoy life to the full, to be a light to those around us and do all we can to make the world a better place. Christians name this impulse 'the work of the Holy Spirit', the personified spirit of God calling us to the best of ourselves. And, of course, the same Holy Spirit calls the church to be a place of wonderment. I don't think that means the rather stunning kind of wonderment we may feel when we hear of rather spectacular phenomena. Instead, we are a wonder because we are countercultural – full of heart for others, love for each other, our communities and for God, and that we are authentic.

God seems to want us to be normal around wonderment. There is a fascinating parallel with that greatest of all astronauts, Neil Armstrong. After his trip to the moon, he disappointed people. He became something of a recluse. He didn't much talk about his experiences. Some said that after having been to the moon he couldn't cope with the routine and normality of life – that wonderment had ruined life for him in some way.

But his children and grandchildren say differently.[9] They lived with Neil. They affirmed that the greatest wonderment he felt was not so much the moon, as seeing the earth from the moon. Its beauty made him aware that it was precious and that we needed to take care of our planet much more effectively. It was a fatherly response. Or perhaps it was more like a son wanting to care for his mother.

Armstrong did not become a bitter recluse, though. Armstrong's kids say that in fact he simply went home and became even more of the person that he always was – thoughtful, musical, a man who always had a song on his lips. Wonder didn't wipe him out, it made him more himself.

Embracing wonderment

What I have found is that Christianity is uniquely placed as the vehicle for embracing wonder. It answers questions about our brokenness, our need for rescue, creation and restored creation, the tough choices we face when we love.

I have come to see that wonder isn't so much a feeling as a way of life. It is open to all, but at its sharpest in the knowledge of the God who made everything and tells our story as part of his.

By now you will know that I am fascinated by flying and always wanted to be an astronaut. Flying seems to me to be almost magical. It is a metaphor for my sometimes-sad soul that has longed to fly. I am not alone. Our planet is full of people who have heard the whisper of wonder and know that it has a deep truth to tell. That truth is not a set of bucket-list experiences. Instead, it is at the heart of the Christian faith – embodied by God among us, who did more than just perform the odd sign and wonder. Jesus calls us to look up and out and have our lives transformed, so we can see and experience wonder all the time. We are also called to see the wonder that is all around us.

It is true, and don't we know it, that each life will contain pain and tragedy, and sometimes that is so bad that we have no idea how we might get through it. But I, at least, have found shards of wonder, of a perspective beyond myself, even in my very lowest times. Our theology and practice of wonder needs to be strong enough to withstand suffering. The example of the saints, both famous and local, is surely a help in such times.

But back to flying. John Gillespie Magee, Jr was a Second World War pilot. He was killed in an accidental mid-air crash in 1941. During his wartime flying career, he only engaged the enemy once and he reported that he had not managed to down any of their fighters. Just a few months before his death he wrote a sonnet called 'High Flight'. His poem is now the official poem of the Royal Air Force and is loved by pilots *and* astronauts alike.

In its delicate beauty, *High Flight* says something about the pilot and astronaut in all of us and our odd sense that this world is not all there is and that God has something amazing in store. Like Gillespie, don't we all want somehow to slip 'the surly bonds of earth', 'put out [our] hand[s]' and touch the gentle, beautiful 'face of God'?

> Oh! I have slipped the surly bonds of Earth
> And danced the skies on laughter-silvered wings . . .
> Put out my hand, and touched the face of God.[10]

Study Questions

It was only with my conversion much later in life that I began to have a hope that wonder was more than just the odd experience and might be a way of life. Perhaps the horizon is an illusion. Wonder is everywhere.

Is wonderment a way of life? Are there ways that it can be something that isn't just a one-off experience?

When you have confidence in God – deep confidence in him – then it is liberating and you don't need to be frightened of others and their reactions. You can be yourself. Think about when God says of Jesus when he is baptized: 'This is my [beloved] . . . with him I am well pleased.' You cannot say 'I am well pleased' without a smile on your face. That reminds us of the divine smile when God looks at us. God is delighted in us. That means that even if we are going through a hard time then there is a bedrock of happiness in our lives. And that means a propensity to joy.

How do you respond to this?

If wonder is not just an experience but a way of being, then it has a bigger story to tell than we thought. Wonder whispers to us that we are both less significant than we think (that we aren't the centre of the universe) and also part of a much bigger story.

Discuss.

Prayer

Lord, we want to know more of your wonder. Help us to find it and to live a life that is shaped by it. Help us to be more childlike in our ability to be amazed and to be curious. Help us to trail light behind us and inspire the people around us. Let us see the wonder in sacrificial love and the ultimate example of that in Jesus.

17

The Church of Wonder

Shortly after Christ's death, as two of his dejected followers are heading home, they meet the Christ on the road right beside them (Luke 24:13–35). What began as an ending of all of what they had hoped for becomes instead a new beginning and a fresh start. Their encounter helps them to see the world afresh and to begin again.

I think that this is a model of the church of wonderment. It is, when all is said and done, a place of fresh hope and new life. The most poetic and mystical of gospels, that of John, explains something of that sense of hope. In it, right at the start of his book, he explains why Jesus is the hope of hopes:

> The true light that gives light to everyone was coming into the world. He was in the world, and though the world was made through him, the world did not recognise him. He came to that which was his own, but his own did not receive him. Yet to all who did receive him, to those who believed in his name, he gave the right to become children of God – children born not of natural descent, nor of human decision or a husband's will, but born of God.

> The Word became flesh and made his dwelling among us. We have seen his glory, the glory of the one and only Son, who came from the Father, full of grace and truth.

> John 1:9–14

In the rich poetry of John, we get a sense of the promise that we *can* be born again. Intriguingly, we also catch a sense of what God among us was actually like from an eyewitness. God in person is 'full of grace and [full of] truth'. These are surely what are at the heart of the church that has wonderment at its very core. If a church is full of truth and grace, then it will seem a wonderful alternative to what the rest of the world so often has to offer.

In our post-Christian society, where many people have never been inside a church and have only heard about Christians and their faith in the media, finding this alternative community that is surprisingly full of joy and purpose is an eye-opener. In Ephesians 1:18, Paul prays for an opening of the eyes of the heart – maybe that's what can happen when a dejected follower of modern consumerism finds their way through our doors. That may be in a glorious cathedral, vibrant Pentecostal church, or silent Quaker meeting. Truth and grace are rare commodities; perhaps they have always been so.

The church is a portal, a way of seeing something, or someone, who can change everything. And we are reminded again of the odd connection with astronauts and spaceships and the transcendent galaxies that are there for our delectation.

It is certainly true that many have worried, and do worry, that the theology that emphasises the majesty of the church has made it too powerful. The chain from this idea led to a church of might and power and an idea that only through darkening the church's doors could we ever be saved. This might generate fear and amazement, but not the kind of wonderment that is astonished that the 'last will be first' (Matt. 19:30) and that God 'humbled himself' (Phil. 2:8).

What follows is not the last word on the wonder-filled church. And I am aware that I don't want to simply picture a church that is full of wonderment to me but doesn't resonate with others. If I invent the ideal church then, of course, it will have a congregation of only one – me.

First principles

Wonder is that sense of amazement when we encounter something beautiful, awesome, remarkable, or unfamiliar. It has a way of helping us to make connections that we hadn't made before and helps us to get out of ourselves and see more clearly the world that we share with others.

I had something of this feeling in my time at the Little Church Around the Corner in mid-town Manhattan. A combination of its incongruous present in the heart of money-town and its incongruous priest suddenly jerked my faith alive. I add to that the beautiful setting of the church itself and its peaceful grounds; the use of the ancient liturgies charmed me and surprised me and gave me a sudden sense of God close at hand.

The church with the Empire State Building in its back garden caught me unawares and at a low ebb, and set me back on the path. I was truly awestruck, and this in a little service with just four people alongside me. What's more, it was the opposite of trendy. It could have survived a power cut, as many of my favourite charismatic churches would struggle to do. It looked like and it smelled like church, and for those seeking refuge there it was just that. I come from a tradition where communion is not the highest priority. But in that small church I was transported by the words of the communion service and the experience of the event.

Others will have the same experience in different churches and places.

For me, the church of wonderment doesn't have to be about signs and wonders – dramatic public healings, direct preaching, or speaking in tongues. But it could be for others. Instead, here are just a few way-markers of the church of wonderment.

The church that is open to be surprised and waylaid

Those early, dejected followers were caught by surprise by the Christ. They were humble enough to speak to a stranger and in doing so had their lives transformed. They didn't have a schedule and were happy to change course.

Perhaps the church of wonderment knows that there is a mystery at the heart of the faith and that sometimes we have to let ourselves be swept away by it. Churches need managing – indeed, the early disciples went through a managerial process when they divided up the tasks of ministry (Acts 6:2–4).

At the very least, wonderment tempts us to be delighted, and if we lose that in church and are engulfed by routine only, where is the room for us all to be surprised?

If we are prepared to be surprised, then it generates a way of doing church that is less hierarchical and less authoritarian. As George Miles tells his photography students – don't think that that photo you set out to get is always the one you are meant to have.

I want my church to be open to being surprised. And for wonderment not to be dependent on some extravagant sign, but in its gentle care for the creation and the people and creatures and plants we share the planet with.

When Edward White stepped out of his spaceship and began his dance of wonder, he realized that the original gravity – original sin – was not the beginning and end of the story. I need church to remind me of that as well.

White was an odd astronaut, because he was more child than scientist or West Point graduate. The church of wonder might need to rediscover the art of playfulness.

The church of questions and adventures

Dear old St Brendan made himself a boat and headed out onto the ocean without a map. Wonder creates a sense of yearning, and that causes us to ask questions and to want to find out more – more about the source of the wonderment we experience.

If a church closes down questions, makes people feel oppressed, or even daft, then it cannot be a place of wonderment.

It is OK not to know every answer. It is better to feel that church is a place of exploration and adventure and quest. I want to set out on a rickety old boat as the ancient saint did and let God put the wind in my sails.

Maybe too, the church of wonderment stretches us to think about what kind of attitude to the world and our community might such a church of wonder have. Does the church allow itself to avert its gaze away from simply fretting about salvation and onto the glorious world around us – nature, the arts, science – and begin to see the really big picture of the glory of the world God has created?

Perhaps we might cut the 45-minute sermon back, and go outside with the congregation and spend some time listening to the birds and wondering about the God who made them. Or spend some time listening to a lonely person and marvelling at their fortitude and bravery.

The ancient Celtic Christians perhaps had their services outdoors – maybe beside the Celtic stone cross. They saw the creation as an expression of God's love and saw no reason to be inside. Why not worship along with their animal friends?

A church that has lightness of touch

When we think of the opposite of places and experiences of wonder, we think of oppressive regimes and authoritarian leaders. We think of regimes that want to squeeze the life and love out of everything. It is no accident that Stalinism was rife with its twin – paranoia.

Church can get to feel paranoid and embattled. Church leaders can become authoritarian, and structures and practices can build up that are deeply unhealthy.

Ah, but let in some wonder and the source of that wonder, and church begins to sing. It begins to be an antidote to the oppressions that are all around us.

> Let in some wonder and the source of that wonder, and church begins to sing.

Let me give you an example. One Sunday, pre-Covid restrictions, our verger came up to do the reading from the Bible. It started badly. She had forgotten her glasses. Having gone back and retrieved them from her handbag, she found it difficult to locate the passage in her Bible. As she started, her phone went off, playing the Benny Hill theme tune – 'Yakety Sax'.[1]

What should I have done as the church leader? How should our church have responded? A telling off? A trip to the vicar's office for some reading practise?

Instead, something beautiful happened. The congregation broke out in applause. They didn't feel sorry for Avril. No; they celebrated her childlike mistake and daft smile and saw something, perhaps, of a God who doesn't seem to mind foolishness.

When I was training, I used to literally sweat anxiety before every service. I was scared of making a mistake. These days I see the understanding of mistakes and the celebration of our unfitness as a mark of a healthy church that understands wonder.

Yes, I know that this kind of approach wouldn't work at a state occasion or a royal wedding. I know that such events cause wonderment. I know that a beautiful church and a beautiful service bring me closer to God. But I wonder as well if a church that feels like the kind of place that you can survive making a mistake, and indeed, might get a round of applause at the end of a good mistake, is perhaps closer to the mark of wonder.

A church that shares the blessing

Church, and a church of wonderment, is a place where we live out that sense of gratitude and goodness and love. This, of course, transcends ecclesiology and denomination.

Church is the most extraordinary thing and, in some ways, makes no sense at all. It is a place that anyone can come to. When done well and properly it is not a bastion of class, race, or a monoculture. In church you will probably meet people you would not associate with elsewhere. It is the very opposite of a club.

We learn sacrificial love from the 'perfecter of [our] faith' (Heb. 12:12) and the church is a wonder when it takes that love out into the world. When we see that sacrificial love in action in our communities, then we are struck by the wonder of love and how it really is what makes life worth living.

We sit at the edge of a new reality, where church has the power to be a place that is more than just an influencer of behaviour. When we get church right, then it is a thing of true wonder.

Study Questions

If a church closes down questions, makes people feel oppressed, or even daft, then it cannot be a place of wonderment.

Discuss.

We learn sacrificial love from the 'perfecter of [our] faith' (Heb. 12:12) and the church is a wonder when it takes that love out into the world. When we see that sacrificial love in action in our communities, then we are struck by the wonder of love and how it really is what makes life worth living.

Discuss.

Prayer

Thank you for the church. Thank you that church is open to all and is a home for the lost, the lonely, the odd, the broken and everything in-between. Help our churches to be places of wonder where people find a new start and fresh hope.
Thank you that there are churches to suit everyone and that the church still proclaims that people are loved and uniquely special. Let us cherish the Holy Church.

NOTES

1 A Life with Wonder

[1] Alister McGrath, *Glimpsing the Face of God* (Oxford: Lion, 2003), pp. 11, 40–41.

[2] For more on Edward White see https://history.nasa.gov/Apollo204/zorn/white.htm (accessed 24 August 2019).

[3] Similar lines can be found on a memorial wall for Alexander Morton (1844–1923) in Darvel, East Ayrshire, Scotland and in the poem *Fra Lippo Lippi* by Robert Browning (1812–1889).

2 The Amazement of Liminal Places and Events

[1] Interview with author, 2019.

[2] https://www.bbc.co.uk/news/uk-48178229 (accessed 6 May 2019).

[3] Luke 17:17,18.

[4] See John 11.

3 Close to Home

[1] Distributed by 20th Century Fox.

4 The Dance of Wonder

[1] By Barry and Marian Sharp, reproduced here with their permission.

[2] Isaiah 6:3.

5 The Farmer and the Donkey

[1] Details in this story have been changed.

7 The Wonder of the Saints

[1] Brother Yun with Paul Hattaway, *The Heavenly Man* (Oxford: Monarch, 2002).

[2] Jackie Pullinger with Andrew Quicke, *Chasing the Dragon* (London: Hodder & Stoughton, 2006; revised edition).

[3] Billy Graham, *Nearing Home* (Nashville, TN: Thomas Nelson, 2013).

[4] See Ephesians 3:18 NRSVA.

[5] Michelle Obama, *Becoming* (New York: Viking, 2018).

[6] N.T. Wright, *The Resurrection of the Son of God* (London: SPCK, 2017).

[7] Revelation 19:7–9.

8 Robert Llewelyn, *The Joy of the Saints* (Springfield, IL: Templegate, 1988), p. xii.

8 The Wintry Grief of the Shoemaker

1 Leo Tolstoy, Nathan Haskell Dole, *Where Love Is, There God Is Also* (Charleston, SC: Nabu Press, 2010). See also https://www.online-literature.com/tolstoy/2892/ (accessed 12 July 2019).

2 Mary Poplin, *Finding Calcutta* (Downers Grove, IL: IVP, 2008).

9 The Little Church Around the Corner

1 The Book of Common Prayer. Reproduced with permission of Cambridge University Press through PLSclear. See https://www.churchofengland.org/prayer-and-worship/worship-texts-and-resources/book-common-prayer/lords-supper-or-holy-communion (accessed 6 January 2021).

10 A Burning Bush and a Holy Place

1 C.S. Lewis, *The Lion, the Witch and the Wardrobe* (London: Geoffrey Bles, 1950).

2 See P. and J. North, *Sacred Space: House of God, Gate of Heaven* (London: Continuum, 2007), pp. 1–9 for an interesting discussion on this.

[3] Joseph Ratzinger, *The Spirit of the Liturgy* (San Francisco, CA: Ignatius Press, 2000).

[4] Interview with the author, 2019.

12 Creation Sings

[1] 'How the UK's first fatal car accident unfolded', https://www.bbc.co.uk/news/magazine-10987606 (accessed 8 January 2021).

[2] See David Adam, *Aidan, Bede, Cuthbert: Three Inspirational Saints* (London: SPCK, 2006), p. 123.

13 The Meal of Wonder

[1] Luke 22:19.

[2] Interview with the author, 2019.

[3] See 1 Corinthians 14.

[4] In conversation with the author, 3 February 2017.

[5] See https://www.churchofengland.org/prayer-and-worship/worship-texts-and-resources/book-common-prayer/lords-supper-or-holy-communion (accessed 7 June 2019).

[6] In conversation with the author, 3 May 2019.

14 Art in a Vacuum

[1] Interview with the author, 2019.

15 The Photographer and the Café

[1] George Miles, Jeremy Millar, *Views Of Matlock Bath* (London: Black Dog Publishing, 2014).

[2] Interview with the author, 2019.

16 Living the Wonderful Life

[1] From the book by Jonathan Swift, *Gulliver's Travels* (London: Benjamin Motte, 1726).

[2] John V. Taylor, *The Go-Between God* (London: SCM, 1972).

[3] Interview with author, June 2019.

[4] *Saint Benedict's Prayer Book* (York: Ampleforth Abbey Press, 2016), p. 39.

[5] Details unfound.

[6] Interview with the author, 2019.

[7] Matthew 3:17.

[8] In conversation with the author, 5 June 2019.

[9] https://www.bbc.co.uk/news/science-environment-48953973 (accessed 3 July 2019).

[10] See https://nationalpoetryday.co.uk/poem/high-flight/ (accessed 9 August 2019).

17 The Church of Wonder

[1] Homer Louis 'Boots' Randolph III (1927–2007).

Our Precious Lives

*Why telling and hearing
stories can save the church*

Steve Morris

Jesus was the master storyteller, powerfully relating
accessible stories to convey the good news, and Steve
Morris calls us to reclaim the art of storytelling in the
church today.

In a world of increasing social fragmentation and
loneliness, this book demonstrates how listening to others
can be transformational in creating a sense of belonging.
Inspiring stories are grounded by practical ideas to put
storytelling at the heart of the church, and questions in
each chapter encourage us all to glimpse more of God,
revel in our uniqueness and realize that we all have
something valuable to offer as his followers.

Underpinned by practical pastoral experience, this is a
book full of quirky and unexpected life stories that open
us up afresh to the beauty of life and our God.

978-1-78893-079-6

The Divine Spark

*Why Celtic wisdom can
refresh the church today*

Steve Morris

Can the ancient model of Celtic Christianity really have
any relevance to our charismatic, evangelical churches?

Celtic Christianity was always on the margins of society,
so looking at how those Christians lived out their faith
can bring real insight into how we model church today.
From slowing down in a busy world, reconnecting with
God through appreciating nature, caring for the planet,
to finding God's presence through mindfulness and
practising whole-life discipleship, there are treasures to be
found that are surprisingly modern and relevant to the
world we live in today.

Discover how the Celtic tradition can revitalize and
reconnect us in our daily walk with God.

978-1-78893-177-9

The Journey Home

*40 Days of
thoughts, prayers and
encouragement
from the Celts*

Steve Morris

Catch a glimpse of the infectious optimism of the Celtic
Christians through these comforting songs, prayers, poems
and devotions as we rediscover the value of community,
feasting, singing and the joy of creation.

The ancient words of the Celts still sparkle with faith in
a personal, ever-present God, whose care is seen in the
details of creation, even when they feel endangered. Like
them, in troubled times, what we long for is a sense of the
nearness of God in our everyday lives.

This inspiring book encourages us to see that our true
home and safety can be found in God.

978-1-78893-195-3

Front-Line Advent

*Daily thoughts, prayers
and encouragement
for Advent*

*Steve Morris
with Barry Hingston*

Advent is a time of reflection. We wonder about the great
theme of darkness and light. We think about what it is to
have faith, and to be peaceful and joyful, even when the
world seems a dangerous and unreliable place. And we
look again at the extraordinary claim that the God who
made the heavens came among us as one of us.

Based on the Lectionary readings for Year B, these daily
thoughts include reflections on beautiful poems, prayers,
explorations of Bible verses and questions to ponder.

Challenging, thought-provoking and inspirational, these
daily reflections will help us to think, pray and be aware of
God's presence in new ways this Advent.

978-1-78893-196-0

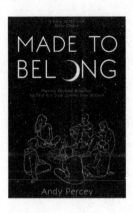

Made to Belong

*Moving beyond tribalism
to find our true
connection in God*

Andy Percey

Where do I belong?

Since our earliest days, humans have sat around tribal fires
and told stories about how we belong. This desire is deeply
built into us and the glow of that fire is still enticing.

We long to 'find our tribe' and to fit in with others like
us. So, even when we scratch the itch of tribalism, why do
we burn for something else? Andy Percey shows us that we
were never made to just fit in; God created us to belong to
him and each other in the truest and deepest way possible.

If you are asking these questions around the fire, this
book is your invitation into relationship, partnership,
companionship and belonging.

978-1-78893-185-4

Infused with Life

*Exploring God's gift of rest in
a world of busyness*

Andy Percey

In a stressful, task-orientated life, we know the importance
of rest, but it is too often pushed out of our busy
schedules.

Join Andy Percey as he reveals that rest is actually God's
good gift to us, provided for us to experience a balance in
our lives that isn't just about rest as recovery, but rest as
harmony with our Creator and the world he has made.

By learning to practise life-giving rhythms of rest, we can
be infused with the very best of the life God freely gives
us.

978-1-78893-065-9

Soul's Scribe

*Connecting your story with
God's narrative*

Kate Nicholas

Each of us has a soul story to tell – the unique story of
how we experience God throughout out lives.

Kate Nicholas expertly takes you on a journey through
the various stages of your life, helping you to see your
soul's story as an adventure full of meaning and purpose,
connecting your tale with the great sweeping arc of God's
eternal narrative.

As you identify the main themes of your life that
connect past and present, you will be able to understand
your life as a coherent whole. And at the end of this
reflective and practical process, you will have the tools to
step out and tell your own story with confidence.

Point others to Jesus as you are empowered to share the
good things God has done for you.

978-1-78893-021-5

Slow Down, Show Up and Pray

Simple shared habits to renew wellbeing in our local communities

Ruth Rice

How can we renew wellbeing in our own lives and in our local communities?

Looking after our mental health has never been so important. Many of us want to find simple ways to help our wellbeing that we can fit into our everyday life.

After suffering her own mental health crisis, Ruth Rice set up the Renew Wellbeing charity, which helps churches open safe spaces to help all attend to their mental and emotional health. Packed full of personal stories, reflective resources and practical guidance, this book will enable you to maintain your own wellbeing and encourage churches to provide Renew spaces that help local communities journey alongside each other to renew wellbeing.

Be present. Be prayerful. Be in partnership.

978-1-78893-183-0

The Christing

Mining the Bible to reveal the extravagant anointing of the Holy Spirit

Paul White

Do you want to fall more in love with Jesus?

The Holy Spirit is the Spirit of Jesus. The awesome power of this 'Christing' is to get the life-giving, oppression-busting, freedom-bringing life of Jesus into the whole world, starting right where we live.

Take a gallop through the scriptures with Paul White and discover the different images used to describe the Holy Spirit. In a fresh and conversational style, peppered with personal stories and the author's own illustrations, you will see how the same dynamic power of God seen throughout the Bible is still available to us today.

Be encouraged to live in a deep, passionate relationship with Jesus. Get ready to release the 'Christing'!

978-1-78893-173-1

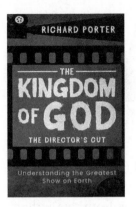

The Kingdom of God – The Director's Cut

Understanding the greatest show on earth

Richard Porter

Jesus taught us to pray for God's kingdom to come. But do we understand what we are praying for and what the kingdom of God really looks like?

Using the analogy of God as the director of the greatest show on earth, Richard Porter shows how the kingdom of God is the overarching storyline throughout the Bible. Each scene, from the people of Israel to Jesus and the early church, reveals kingdom truths that impact the church today.

As the story unfolds, you will understand why Jesus proclaimed the message of the kingdom and why it is indeed good news for our towns, our cities, our homes and our families.

978-1-78893-169-4

We trust you enjoyed reading this book from Authentic. If you want to be informed of any new titles from this author and other releases you can sign up to the Authentic newsletter by scanning below:

Online:
authenticmedia.co.uk

Follow us: